Retirement

A Journey not a Destination

Reflections by a Traveler

One Year down the Road

Katherine P. Stillerman

For My Family

Table of Contents

Introduction

August 2011

At five o'clock in the afternoon, a year ago, I closed my office door as principal of East Iredell Middle School and made my way to the car, officially beginning my retirement. In the thirty years prior, every day, excluding weekends, holidays and sick days, I spent the hours between eight am and five pm in one of North Carolina's one hundred thirty-nine local education agencies (LEA), expending my energy and expertise to provide a free, public, universal education to the children of the district I served. I began as a teacher, and worked in several LEA's in the eastern part of the State. Later, I worked in curriculum and served as a building level administrator in three LEA's in the Triad.

Regardless of the location, the routine was pretty much the same. The sun would be rising in the east when I arrived in the morning to greet the staff and students at around seven-thirty; and, it would be setting in the west as I crossed the vacant parking lot to my car and departed for home. As the earth rotated and the sun made its arc across the sky, marking the beginning and ending of each day, I remained stationary, within the walls and compounds of the school, performing my various duties and fulfilling my various responsibilities.

There were, of course, times when I would leave the building for administrative meetings, workshops, and other district-related events. Occasional luncheons and opportunities to network with colleagues took me out of the building. However, for the most part, my days were spent right there within the walls of the school, supervising students, working with teachers, and meeting with parents.

In a middle school, there is never a dull moment and every day is full of surprises. I often became so absorbed in the issues at hand that I would lose track of time and become oblivious to what was going on in the outside world. Frequently, when I returned home at night, my husband Bill would comment on how hot or rainy or cold it had been. I had to admit that I had remained inside all day and not noticed the weather at all.

For thirty years, my time from at least eight am to five pm was encumbered and my location determined by the LEA to which I was under contract. That represents about 57,600 hours, almost all spent within the walls of public schools in the State of North Carolina. Admittedly, I chose the path of public school education and I gained much satisfaction from my work, along with the frustration, tedium, and redundancy that comes with any job. Job satisfaction and fulfillment notwithstanding, that is a whole heck of a lot of time to spend in one place! Now, after thirty years, the State of North Carolina was, in essence, handing over those hours to me, as well as providing me with a monthly retirement check sufficient to maintain my current standard of living.

I walked across the asphalt parking lot, vapor rising from the summer heat, opened the car door, and laid my sweater over the seat to keep from singeing the back of my legs. I started the ignition, slid back the moon roof, and rolled down all the windows. As I popped the transmission into Drive and proceeded out of the parking lot for the last time, a rush of sensations arose with the hot summer air. I felt like a kid let out of school for the summer; like a bird out of a cage; like an inmate freed from prison (bad analogy); like a ship without an anchor.

As I sped away, the question that had nagged at me since I finalized a retirement date returned: What in the world would I do with the forty-plus hours a week that had been given back to me? I had determined that my first project would be to spend time searching for the answer to that question and writing about it. What follows is an account of my journey one year out.

Retirement Project: How it all Began

A significant number of my friends and colleagues in the Iredell Statesville system had either retired or were fast approaching the day when they would do so. Most of them had begun as teachers when they were twenty-one and fresh out of college. Those who had worked continuously, without a break, were eligible for full North Carolina retirement benefits by the age of fifty-one; and, they would only be fifty-six if they stayed on an extra five years to reach their thirty-five year tenure. Many of them were beginning to suffer stress and burnout from being at it for so long and had started to consider their options for retirement.

Although I had begun my teaching career at twenty-one like the others, I dropped out for a number of years to raise a family. When I returned, I found myself a decade older than these youngsters with thirty plus years of service. The break had energized me, and I was not yet suffering from the job stress and burnout that many of them were beginning to experience. Thus, I was sixty-two before I thought seriously about winding down my career, and sixty-five when I finally set a retirement date, which fell one month short of my sixty-sixth birthday.

Often, when this particular group of colleagues got together, either informally or at district gatherings, the topic of retirement would dominate the conversation. In the earlier years, I listened with detached interest, as those who had officially set their *going out* date would share their plans. At some point in the conversation, someone would always ask, "What convinced you to make the final decision to set your retirement date? ".

Invariably, the one questioned would respond, "I just knew that it was time." And then, he or she would almost always add, "And, you will know too." Based on the frequency with which that advice was repeated, I assumed that since I did not "just know," it must not be time; and so, I kept on working. Eventually, I discovered that piece of conventional wisdom to be dead-on right. One day, I did "just know it was time," and I set my retirement date for August 1, 2011.

At that point, I became more invested in the retirement conversations and more interested in learning about how my respected colleagues were managing the impending transition in their lives. They had been the ones who had mentored me and helped me when I resumed my career as an educator, as well as the ones with whom I collaborated and from whom I sought advice when I became a more experienced principal. Naturally, I assumed that they would have gained some wisdom beyond my own that they could impart. What I found was that they were just as much in the dark as I was.

Although opinions and sentiments varied, a mood of uncertainty clouded our discussions, and I found the talk to be depressingly negative, especially as it became increasingly relevant to my own situation. One of the more prevalent views I heard expressed went something like this: "I'd be okay for about six months, but after I got my fill of sleeping late and watching old movies, I'd start to go stir crazy. I already have my thirty-five years in, but if I didn't have to get up and go to work, I wouldn't have anything to do." Those who held this view seemed to think of retirement as a life sentence, an event to be dreaded and delayed until they became too sick or too old to continue working. They spoke of it with foreboding and gloom.

Opposite the view of *retirement as a life sentence,* but equally prevalent in our conversations, was one that I have come to regard as the *retirement as a get-out-of-jail-free pass.* Those who espoused this view usually focused upon the drudgery of work life, emphasized the burnout they were experiencing, and measured time in terms of the days, hours, and minutes left before they were eligible to cash in their chips and get away. "I have two years, twenty days, and seven hours until I can get out of this place."

Let me emphasize here that my colleagues and I were not generally regarded as negative people. We were proven professionals, who had built distinguished careers in education and made a significant difference, both individually and collectively, in the Iredell Statesville district. We strove to be motivators, visionaries, and leaders of change. We had all fully bought into the district vision *To ignite a passion for learning in all students*. We all professed our commitment to continuous growth and learning for ourselves and for others. We claimed we believed in learning as a lifelong venture. However, our conversations about retirement presented shortsighted visions, devoid of any element of continuous growth in which we all professed to believe.

The prevailing group wisdom from our conversations appeared to be*: Work until you drop, or retire and be bored to death*; or, *Put in your time, get out when you can, and take what they owe you.* And, whichever option you choose, *You will know when it is time to go.* Was this really the best we could come up with? I did not think it was, but at that time, I did not have anything better to offer. I was not satisfied with either vision and I was determined to find one that incorporated my core belief in continuous growth and learning into my own retirement plans. Over the next few months, that vision began to emerge.

In March, I flew to New York City for a cousins' club reunion and I picked up the book *Happiness Project* by Gretchen Rubin at the airport gift shop. I was attracted to the title because I had recently finalized my retirement date for August 1, 2011, and was thinking a great deal about the impact my decision would have on my own happiness and well-being.

Rubin writes about the changes she made, resulting from a mid-life malaise that prompted her to dedicate an entire year to seeking the meaning of happiness. She began her journey with extensive research on the subject, drawing from the fields of philosophy, religion, psychology, autobiography, and popular culture. Building on what she had learned, she wrote resolutions that identified what brought her *joy, satisfaction, and engagement*, as well as *guilt, anger, boredom, and remorse*. Her resolutions became action steps for converting her new theories into everyday practice. Her goal was to master one resolution per month, moving on to the next resolution at the end of the month, and maintaining the one practiced previously. She blogged about her progress, shared her unique experiences, and encouraged others to create their own path to finding a happy and joyful life.[1]

Rubin provided a helpful model for managing change that I could relate to in preparing for the transition that was about to take place in my own life. It was appealing to me to think of retirement as a project, a work in progress. The book planted the seed of a plan to use the model for her *Happiness Project* to create my own *Retirement Project*. My resolve to implement the project strengthened during the weekend in New York as we cousins carried on our lively dialogues over gourmet dinners, Mid-Town shopping, and a Broadway play.

In the course of sharing experiences and catching one another up on our respective family activities, the topic of my retirement naturally arose. The majority of the cousins, all of us Baby Boomers, were retired, semi-retired, or beginning to plan for it. As we discussed my August 1 date, a sense of tentativeness and discomfort pervaded the conversation, echoing what I recognized as my own squeamishness about the subject. It was similar to the feeling one gets whenever a topic like menopause in mixed groups, or even cancer, comes up. I had experienced those feelings before, but did not realize how strong or universally shared they were.

It was surprising to me as well to sense the angst associated with the questions posed about my plans, as well as my responses to them. Shades of earlier conversations with my work colleagues emerged and the image of retirement as a life sentence resurfaced. Someone asked, "What are you going to do with all that time?" and another wanted to know, "Will you stop working completely or do you plan to do something else?" Still another cut to the heart of it when she posed, "How are you going to spend the rest of your life?" I felt inadequate to reply and weakly responded, "I'm not sure. I don't know. That's something I'm working on." I was puzzled over the power that this word held over us that made it so difficult to talk about, when we were perfectly at ease in conversing about every other subject under the sun.

I have since concluded that what makes us uncomfortable is the change that retirement symbolizes. This insight came to me after reading Robert Raines' *A Time to Live: Seven Steps of Creative Aging*, a book which I would discover shortly after my return from New York, and one that would become an invaluable resource to me. Raines explains that we begin to think about our mortality as we pass into the stage of life he calls the *elder season*. We start to measure our life not from its beginning but to its end. That is unsettling and even scary. Raines continues that there is a hopeful side as well. Thanks to improved health care and extended lifespans, most of my generation will enter retirement in the spring of the elder season. We are likely to have many years, and if we are fortunate, the good health and financial resources, to re-invent ourselves and to live happily and productively throughout our elder years.[2]

Raines identifies seven tasks of creative aging for successful passage into the elder season. (1) *Waking Up* to recognize our mortality. (2) *Embracing Sorrow* of ourselves and others to deepen our humanity and make us more compassionate. (3) *Savoring Blessedness* by remembering how you have been, are, and can be a blessed and blessing person. (4) *Re-Imagining Work* by reviewing and revising how you will contribute to society, give your gift, live out your purpose in the years ahead. (5) *Seeking Forgiveness* by clearing the decks of your relationships to live with an unburdened heart. (6) *Nurturing Intimacy* by deepening your connections with others, God, nature, and yourself. (7) *Taking on the Mystery* by accepting life and death and exploring the meaning of your life with thanksgiving and hope. I would incorporate several of these tasks into my retirement project in the coming months as my vision for retirement evolved. [3]

Though I still had many questions, I left New York invigorated by the city, the cousins, and a newly gained perspective on my future. My vision for retirement as a project to find happiness and fulfillment was taking shape, and it was looking more like a journey than a destination; more like a construction site than a memory garden; more like a beginning than an ending.

I understand now that retirement is, in reality, both an end and a beginning; and, I realize that both aspects need to be given their due. Robert Raines devotes an entire chapter to the task of re-imagining work. He challenges us *to explore our work, which not only takes most of our waking hours and energy, but is also a major vehicle for our creativity and a container of our identity* and to *re-imagine* our work life as we make our way through the passage of the elder season. However, he also encourages us to take pride in the contributions we have made through our *ten thousand hours* of work that are now coming to an end. This is all a part of facing and dealing with each of the passages or stages of life creatively, in order that we might grow and benefit from change.[4]

In retrospect, I probably should have lingered a bit more than I did to honor the thirty years of work as an educator that I had completed and to acknowledge the career that was formally coming to an end. Instead, I chose not to announce my retirement to the faculty until school was almost out, and I made it abundantly clear to my administrative staff that I wanted no fuss made over my leaving. I even declined to attend the annual district retirement dinner.

My reaction was partially motivated by a need for privacy as well as a strong aversion to being cast into the limelight. It was also evidence that I was in denial about what was about to happen. Whatever the case, it was my loss and, in hindsight, I would have handled things differently. But, I was also caught up in my new vision to embrace retirement as a project to find happiness and fulfillment in my elder season, and I was eager to get started on the journey. About that decision, I have no regrets.

I had no sophisticated tracking system to guide me through the passage into this new territory. However, I had recently developed a personal mission statement, which would serve as a compass to keep me pointed in the right direction. Short and compact, like a real compass, it is light, easy to carry, and has four basic points: *To Live*

Purposefully; To Love Unconditionally; To Learn Perpetually; To Laugh Frequently. At the same time, it incorporated all of my core values and beliefs, and I trusted that it would serve me well on my journey.

Live Purposefully refers to my desire to have a meaningful life, to make a difference in the world and to act with integrity, according to my values and ethical and spiritual beliefs. It encompasses everything from how I care for my body and my health, to how I manage my personal possessions, to how I care for the environment, and to how I relate to my family and friends and colleagues in the workplace, and to strangers and people in need.

Love Unconditionally refers to my intention to embrace family, friends, colleagues, and strangers in a non-judgmental manner, and to refrain from placing restrictions and pre-requisites on my love and acceptance of others. It also speaks to my desire for transparency in my relationships, as well as my intention to recognize the commonalities of humanness rather than the differences.

Learn Perpetually. I believe that there is no such thing as standing still in life. One is either growing and changing or shriveling up and withering away. I intend to remain a lifelong learner; to keep my mind, my spirit, and all of my senses open to the world for as long as I am able.

Laugh Frequently speaks to my desire to appreciate and savor life; to remember not to take myself too seriously; to get caught up in the moment; to occasionally lose track of time; to stop and smell the roses.

I decided to use Gretchen Rubin's *Happiness Project* as a framework for organizing my own *Retirement Project*. Like Rubin, I planned to spend a year seeking the meaning of happiness and fulfillment for my life; and, like her, I would record and share my progress month by month. I began with Rubin's recommended process of identifying what brings you joy, satisfaction, and engagement, as well as what brings you guilt, anger, and boredom, and then proceeded to the next step of developing resolutions and creating concrete actions to boost my happiness and fulfillment. I came up with my own set of ten resolutions, five of which easily fit Rubin's model of being concrete and measurable, as well as specific and realistic.

Take Time to Travel. I knew from experience that travel always boosts my happiness and broadens my perspective. My action was to plan a trip to the UK.

Control My Possessions (before they get control of me). I was drowning in *stuff* and that made me very unhappy. My action would be to organize and de-clutter my closets and shelves in every room of the house.

Write to Publish. I love to write and I looked forward to having time to pursue that interest and to develop my skills as a writer. My action would be to write about my first year of retirement and publish it in a blog.

Get Fit and Healthy. Nothing depresses me more than being out of shape. When I do not feel good about my physical appearance and wellbeing, it clouds every other aspect of my life. My actions would be to maintain a daily exercise regimen and drop at least ten pounds.

Read, Read, Read. I am a slow reader and have a memory like a sieve. When I was working full time, I never had enough time for reading books or articles of personal interest for all the other demands that took precedence in my work life. Often, I would start a book, get interrupted, and by the time I got back to it, had lost interest or forgotten what I had previously read. My action would be to read daily and keep a response log of everything I read. I intended to read for fun; read to learn; and to read with the eye of a writer.

The last five resolutions do not fit as neatly into Rubin's process as the first five. In fact, they are not so much resolutions as they are attitudes or insights that I was convinced I must learn and acquire in the process of finding happiness and fulfillment.

Two of these resolutions came directly from Robert Raines' tasks for creative aging in his book entitled *A Time to Live*, to which I have previously referred. The other arose out of general insights gained from Raines' book as well as from my personal mission statement. Because of their abstract nature, I struggled over how to word each one precisely, and had great difficulty generating specific actions for measuring progress. In the end, I included them as resolutions along with the first five, with the expectation of discovering the requisite actions and measures through the process of learning by doing as the year progressed.

Embrace Loss and Sorrow. I was struggling with unresolved grief over my father's death in December of 2010, and I was also becoming aware of the loss I would feel when my retirement date arrived. I was unsure of what to do about it, except that I did find Robert Raines' words about embracing my feelings rather than glossing over them to be comforting, and I resolved to spend time contemplating and reflecting on how to accomplish that task.

Re-Define Work. Although my career as an administrator was ending, I knew that my work was not done. I wanted to spend time reflecting upon my relationship to my work and how I have regarded it over the past thirty years, and to determine how those views would need to be altered to fit my life in the elder season.

Journey Inward. I had sadly neglected the spiritual side of my life and felt that if I were to find meaning and purpose in the elder season, I would need to spend time working on Raines' tasks of *Waking Up to Face Mortality* and of *Taking on the Mystery* by accepting the meaning of life and death with thanksgiving and hope. For starters, I wanted to take a critical look at my love-hate relationship with the institutional church, and to determine its relevance to my life as both a source of spiritual nourishment and community, and a place where I might contribute to and serve the needs of others. My first step would be to end my twenty-year status as a church dropout by joining a Sunday school class.

Re-Connect. During the twelve years that I commuted to Statesville, I had become unplugged from my own community of Winston-Salem. I had dropped out of church, and, with our sons up and grown, I no longer had any involvement with the local schools. Long workdays prevented my helping out with the various community agencies and causes during the week, and on the weekends, I needed time to rest and complete leftover work from school. Outside of work, my social life was limited primarily to family gatherings and time that Bill and I were able to spend together on weekends. My circle of friends had narrowed and I hardly even knew my neighbors. I wanted to get out and become re-acquainted with the people and places of Winston-Salem. I wanted to find outlets for serving and giving back some of the time and energy previously spent elsewhere.

Wander and Explore New Pathways. One perk that retirement promised was the luxury of time to engage in new pursuits and interests. I was weary of being bound to pre-determined schedules and agendas, many of which were not of my own making or under my control. I wanted my retirement project to make room for side trips and distractions, as well as time to wander down untraveled roads in search of sources for happiness and fulfillment yet undiscovered.

Initially, I followed Gretchin Ruben's *Happiness Project* model by establishing a blog, which I called *The Retirement Project,* to record my progress as I journeyed through the year of reflection, research, and re-invention, in search of happiness and fulfillment. I became a regular blogger through January, when I abandoned it to pursue a variety of other writing-related projects that did not lend themselves to a blogging format. I have included some of those in later chapters.

It was at that point that I began to consider the notion of publishing my writing in book form, as a personal memoir of my journey through the first year of retirement. To convey a sense of chronology and progression through the year, I would create a chapter for each month and write about the course of my journey during that span of time. That worked well for the first few months, when my journeys and wanderings were of a literal and outward nature, each with a measureable beginning and end, each informed by an itinerary or guidebook that spelled out the intended destination. My trip in August to the UK; the project undertaken in September to de-clutter my house; and, my journey in October down the road to better fitness are all cases in point.

However, as the year progressed, my journey took an inward turn as I examined my spiritual and philosophical underpinnings, and reflected upon how I would travel the metaphorical road ahead. We can rarely measure our inward journeys chronologically, at least not in arbitrary increments of calendar months. For example, in April, I included my writings about re-defining work for the elder season. The topic of work is one that had been on my mind throughout the year and could not be isolated to April alone; however, for continuity sake I put it in one chapter. In the end, I abandoned the chapter-for-each-month organization, although I did preserve the chronology where it made sense to do so.

In the final analysis, I organized the book topically, with each chapter focusing on one of the resolutions I had written to inform and guide my Retirement Project. Each of the resolutions fit nicely into that format, with one exception. My resolution *to Re-connect* became a recurring theme in my life that I chose to address throughout the book, rather than in one discrete chapter. Thus, I ended up with nine chapters focused on resolutions rather than ten.

A Drop in the Bucket

I derived a great deal of satisfaction and sense of personal accomplishment from completing this book. It has been one of my lifelong goals to write and publish my work. However, there is nothing original or extraordinary in this account of my journey into the first year of retirement. Many of the truths I discovered are self-evident ones; and, much of what I have written simply affirms or rephrases what other people have said before. Memoirs like mine are a dime a dozen; and, there is a host of people who have written about their life circumstances that are of much greater global consequence than mine.

However, I believe that there is something unique and important about my story that transcends the realm of personal accomplishment. It is important because it adds to the corpus of narratives that an increasing number of people like me are writing as we move into the elder season of life and realize just how long that season could be.

Clearly, we have entered a new era of lengthening lifespans. It is no longer a rarity to hear of someone celebrating a one hundredth birthday. In fact, centenarians are the fastest growing segment of the population in terms of age.[5] My husband Bill tells me that at Brookridge Retirement Community, right here in Winston-Salem, there is a resident who just celebrated her one-hundred sixth birthday, and another resident who is still throwing bridge parties at one hundred two. Bill estimates that there have been at least twenty-five centenarians across the state residing in one of the five campuses operated by Baptist Retirement Homes of North Carolina, Inc.[6] The Social Security Administration estimates that as many as half of the girls born today will live to one hundred.[7]

My generation, the Baby Boomers, now faces retirement with increasing odds that we could live to one hundred. This gives a new sense of urgency to the old retirement question "What are you going to do with the rest of your life?" We are charting new territory here that most of our grandparents and even parents never entered.

Where is the map? How do we plan for this journey? Who or what will be our guide? These are questions that I believe we must answer individually to ensure quality and meaning in the elder season of life, regardless of how many years that may be. They are also questions that we, as a generation, need to answer collectively, to ensure that our skills and wisdom are recycled and used for the good of society rather than squandered on inactivity and dis-involvement.

The contents of this book contribute at least one drop in the bucket that I hope will someday carry to the children and grandchildren of my generation the conventional wisdom and models of how to live with purpose and meaning all the way to the end of life.

CHAPTER 1

Resolution: *Take Time to Travel*

My eagerness to travel and see the world has been dampened by a strong aversion to flying, resulting from an inherited propensity for motions sickness. It was passed down to me from my dad, who could not even stand on a floating boat dock for more than a few minutes without becoming woozy from the motion. I get that same sensation from flying.

Taking off in a plane makes my ears pop, my head swim, my palms sweat, and my heart race. By the time we reach cruising altitude, I am as disoriented as a drunk driver who has been pulled over and made to walk a straight line. The queasiness does not subside until the wheels of the plane hit the tarmac and the force of gravity on my body is normalized.

I could probably minimize the effect of the vertigo if I would take a Dramamine or a sleeping pill and try to relax during the trip. However, my aversion to flight is also fueled by an overwhelming resistance to loss of control.

I feel compelled to remain alert at all times so that I might personally detect the slightest irregularity in the flight pattern or the minutest change in the stability of the plane. I simply cannot quiet my mind and stop it from backseat driving, or in this case, co-piloting. The slightest tilt in the plane or change in its motion makes me feel like a cat, flipped over on its back, clawing to get its feet back under it.

Once, on a flight from Greensboro to Atlanta, I became alarmed over the fact that, after only twenty minutes in the air, the nose of the plane seemed to be tilting forward and that we might possibly be going down. I gripped the arms of the seat, closed my eyes, and took charge in my imaginary cockpit. Through sheer mind control, I was determined to level that plane; however, we continued nose down, to lose altitude.

Momentarily, the fasten-seat-belt signs lit up and the captain came on the intercom to announce our descent, and to tell us that we would soon be landing in Atlanta. It turns out, the flight was so short that the plane only had time to get up to cruising altitude, level off, and head back down. By the time I realized that, I had already prepared for the worst and had accepted the fact that we would inevitably crash and that my remains would be scattered across north Georgia.

When one is unable to give up control and trust the pilot and crew to do their jobs, any flight can become exhausting. It is tiring enough to be on duty and mentally fly the plane on a short trip, but when it comes to a trans-Atlantic flight, that is another story altogether. But let's face it, if you want to see the world, you have to fly over the pond, or take a ship. Choose your poison. Mine is flying.

For years, I refused to go anywhere unless I could walk, drive, take the train, or take the bus. Because of my fear of flying, I missed-out on many wonderful opportunities to travel. In 1996, our son Todd went off to Harvard Law School. Cambridge, Massachusetts is seven hundred eighty-one miles from Winston-Salem, and it is the farthest distance away that any of our four children had ever lived.

I knew that we would want to visit Todd and to have him show us all around the Boston area. I was also an over-protective mom who did not like the idea that I could not get to any one of my children in a matter of a few hours. The trip by car is almost fourteen hours as opposed to a flight from Winston-Salem to Logan Airport in Boston, which takes about three. Given those options, I decided to get over my phobia and never again let my fear of flying deprive me of the opportunity to be with the people I love, or to travel and see new places.

I have not completely conquered my fears, but I have made great headway in tolerating flight as a necessary mode of transportation. In 2002, I took a delightful trip to Italy with sons John and Harry, visiting Rome, Siena, Venice, and Florence; and, I survived the fourteen-hour flight, my first across the Atlantic. On subsequent flights, I managed to watch in-flight movies and even nod off for brief periods.

I have improved in my ability to give up control and trust the pilot to get us to our destination, with an occasional lapse into mental back seat driving, or co-piloting. On a crowded eleven-hour flight back from Paris, the year after 9/11, I could not force myself to take in the latest movies or listen to music or sleep, as all of the other passengers were doing. Instead, I watched the small GPS screen attached to the back of the seat in front of me track our flight over the Atlantic, the tiny image of the plane inching its way toward land. It was like staring at the hands of a clock for six hours. But, by God, I stayed vigilant; and, I would have been among the first to know if an engine had malfunctioned or a terrorist tried to take over the plane. As much as I love to visit faraway places, and to become acquainted with different languages and cultures and people, it is still the *getting there* that stands in the way.

I have kept my resolution not to allow my aversion to flying to stand in the way of being with the people I love and of visiting the places I want to see. When I found out that our son Robert would be spending the summer in London, serving a three-month internship with the Bloomsbury Baptist Church, I knew it was time to plan another trip. With retirement right around the corner, I would have the time as well as the motivation to travel.

On August 4, while all of my former fellow principals were gathering for the annual four-day ISS Leadership Academy, I was busy getting out of town. My son Harry and I boarded a plane from Charlotte to Gatwick Airport for a twelve-day trip to the UK. We met up with Robert, Harry's twin brother, for a tour of London, Edinburgh, and Stratford-Upon-Avon. I kept a journal of the trip and took many pictures, which I published on my blog at amostretired@blogspot.com.

Travel Log

Pre-trip Jitters. I developed a case of pre-trip jitters about a week before leaving on my trip to the UK. It had been several years since I had flown extensively and I was nervous about navigating through security and customs as well as dreading the eight-hour flight. As an avid viewer of the 7:00 o'clock evening news, I recalled Brian Williams' coverage of heightened security measures at airports, the indignity suffered by passengers required to undergo body searches, and, most troubling of all, the incidents of pilots falling asleep. Falling asleep? I had never dreamed of that possibility. I always thought that once you were up in the air, that was the safest time.

I packed and repacked my suitcase, trying to decide what to take and what to leave behind, ignoring the advice of travel guru Rick Steves to pack only the things that you will absolutely need, and then take half of that. "Remember," Rick says. "Anything you pack, you will lug around with you everywhere you go." He was so right, as I later recalled while crammed onto the London Tube at rush hour, loaded down with all of my precious belongings that I could not leave behind.

As the average temperature in Winston-Salem was ninety-five, and more like ninety-eight in my bedroom where I was assembling and trying on mix-and-match ensembles and practice packing, I was having a terrible time imagining that it could possibly be seventy-two degrees in London and that I would even be able to tolerate a light sweater. Consequently, I packed way too few warm things, reasoning that I could always layer up if I got cold. Recalling that we were also going to Scotland where it would be even a few degrees cooler and that we would be outside at night when we attended the Military

Tattoo, I threw in my dingy yellow fleece hoodie at the last minute and ended up living in it for the entire trip. It is now on my *things to burn* list.

Also fueling this case of pre-trip jitters was a nagging fear of the baggage getting lost and me arriving in London without clean underwear and a change of clothes. From past experience with overseas flights, I realized that if that happened, I would be forced to spend the first few days of my trip wandering around London in my wrinkled black jersey pants and white ballet top. I could visualize that top, dribbled with marinara sauce from the pasta dish served in the cardboard TV dinner tray on the plane. The blouse would have gotten stained when I lifted a piece of pasta to my mouth on a rickety plastic fork at the very moment that the three-hundred pound passenger in the seat in front of me would have decided to recline into my lap, forcing the fork- full of food down my shirt.

To prevent such a catastrophe from ruining my first days in London and to make sure that I would not be deprived of anything I might need on the eight-hour flight, I determined to carry on board with me a change of clothes and shoes, makeup, medication, a tiny sewing kit, first aid items, and little samples of anything I might need, in addition to Kindle, camera, cell phone, passport, US and

British currency, credit cards, and all confirmations and reservations for hotels and events. If I had been traveling into the wilds of Borneo, I could not have been more prepared.

In my pre-trip obsession, I visited the US Airways website and read everything I could about getting ready for a trans-Atlantic flight. The airlines had enforced additional security measures since my last trip abroad, as Brian Williams so helpfully pointed out, and I wanted to make sure to update myself on all of them. I carefully followed all instructions to separate out liquids and gels and have them ready for inspection at the security gate. I crammed all of my tiny samples of toothpaste, cleanser, moisturizer, eye drops, and antiseptic hand cleaner into a plastic bag where they would be visible. Then, I made certain that a ten day supply of each of the aforementioned were packed into the bag that I would be checking, so that I would be amply supplied for the remainder of the trip, if and when I became reunited with my suitcase.

By the time August 4 finally arrived, I had completely worn myself out in preparation and anticipation. Fatigue may be just the cure for the pre-trip jitters. Having made it successfully through all of the boarding procedures, and seated on the plane ready for take-off, I had only enough energy left to consider briefly the terrible possibility that the pilot might fall asleep and we might go plunging into the Atlantic Ocean in the dark of night, never to be heard from again.

Shortly, I heard the comforting Southern drawl of the pilot, briefing us on the flight and announcing that we would be taking off in the next ten minutes. I relaxed into my seat and thought, *This boy's not going to be falling asleep. He is going to get us there without a hitch. All I have to do now is make it through the first ten minutes of the flight—they say the takeoff and landings are the most dangerous. Once we get in the air I can relax.*

And then, my attractive young seatmate, who I later discovered was on her way to London to King's College for her first year of medical school, turned to me and said, "Don't you just love to fly? I especially like the take-off. It gives me such a rush." And I said, "Oh, yes," and closed my eyes while we lifted off.

The flight was long but smooth as silk. When we began our descent to Gatwick Airport a little after 7:00 am London time, a twinge of the flying jitters returned and I braced myself for the landing—the second most dangerous part of the trip. We touched down with featherlike motion. It was such a gentle landing that it must have impressed the rest of the passengers as well because a spontaneous round of applause broke out in the cabin as we taxied off the runway. That Southern boy knew how to fly a plane!

With feet planted on terra firma and loaded down with the baggage that had miraculously not gotten lost, Harry and I set out for Victoria Station, where we met up with Robert, who was a sight for sore eyes after being gone for three months, living in London and working at Bloomsbury Church. With that reunion, we began our tour of London, with Robert as our guide.

Friday, August 5. We enjoyed lunch at one of Robert's favorite places across from the British Museum, which was just a block from our hotel as well as Bloomsbury Church. We walked over to the museum after lunch and managed to locate the Rosetta Stone and wander around in the Great Court for a few minutes before jet lag overtook us. Harry and I headed back to our hotel for a short rest, while Robert went to get his suitcase and travel things.

When Robert returned, he was eager to begin showing us all of the nearby sights. He took us on a walking tour of Covent Garden, the Opera House, Piccadilly Circus, and Trafalgar Square. We finished the day at a great French restaurant and then crashed for the night in our rooms at the Radisson.

Saturday, August 6. We headed out for a walking tour of the city. It was a glorious day—cool, clear, and sunny. After taking a full English breakfast in the gardens of Victoria Embankment, we walked our legs off, visiting site after site along the Thames.

In one of the gardens at St. Paul's Cathedral, we were taking pictures of an onyx statue of St. Thomas a Becket, who was murdered on the altar of Canterbury Cathedral in 1170, for defending the rights of the Church over the authority of his friend, King Henry II. We overheard a British mother explaining to her small son the martyrdom of the saint: "He and King Henry (II) were best friends and the king got very cross with him--and he had him killed."

Robert pointed out a bit of British humor on the sign for Hung, Drawn and Quartered, a pub below the flat where he stayed with Margaret and Keith, in the City of London.

> *I went to see Major General Harrison hung, drawn, and quartered.*
> *He was looking as cheerful as any man could in that condition.*
> Samuel Pepys, 13 October 1660

Journey's End

On Saturday night, Robert had arranged for us to go with two of his Bloomsbury friends to dinner and a play. He had bought us all tickets to *Journey's End*, at the Duke of York Theater, a small auditorium with an intimate atmosphere. We had marvelous seats at center stage, only a few rows back, which enhanced our sense of being right there in the middle of the action. The drama is set in a World War I bunker in St. Quentin, France, as a group of British officers awaits their day of reckoning and a young Captain Stanhope tries to galvanize his men who are preparing to raid the enemy across No Man's Land. The play is suspenseful, moving, and darkly funny, as it reveals the range of emotions and responses of the soldiers facing their fate, determined by the rigid and inept decisions made from the command center.

Coincidentally, I had recently read several books set in the era surrounding the Great War that provided a context for the play and heightened its impact for me as a viewer. One was *Colonel Roosevelt,* the third of Edmund Morris's brilliant trilogy on Theodore Roosevelt. It explores TR's life after the presidency amidst events leading the United States into a much-debated decision to abandon President Wilson's position of neutrality and join the war on the side of England and France, against Germany. TR, who repeatedly denounced Wilson for his refusal to prepare the military for eventual conflict, believed that war was inevitable and necessary. TR threw his support behind the war effort and encouraged his sons to enlist in officer training and volunteer to lead in the action.

From Ken Follette's *Fall of Giants,* a *fascinating epic that traces the lives of five interrelated families and the impact of war and its aftermath on their lives,* I developed a sense of the gruesome reality of trench warfare and the magnitude of suffering caused by a war that took fifteen million lives and imposed twenty million casualties.[1] Follette does a masterful job of conveying the senselessness of brave soldiers marching off to be slaughtered, pawns in a war game controlled by stubborn and inept decision makers using outmoded and faulty war strategy. He personalizes the losses for the reader as he tells of the tiny Welch mining town in the aftermath of a major battle on the Western front, where one of the main character's family trembled at their door as they were passed by and spared from one of the hundreds of dreaded telegrams that were being delivered to their friends and neighbors informing them that a son had been sacrificed in the battle.

Two of the books I read dealt with the decade after the Armistice in 1918, and the disillusionment and trauma and loss experienced by an entire generation impacted by the Great War. *In Paris Wife*, a novel set in the late 1920's, Paula McLain explores the lingering impact of the war upon the lives of the lost generation of artists and writers living in Paris, told from the perspective of Ernest Hemmingway's first wife Hadley Richardson. In *Winter Ghosts*, Kate Mosse writes about a young man seeking to deal with the loss of the brother he idolized, more than a decade after he went off to war and never returned. These two books heightened my awareness of the lingering effects of war and the long-term impact on its victims.

These recently read works sensitized me to the intricacies of the drama, and I was profoundly affected by its content. The play ended, predictably, with the officers, fully armed, rushing out of the bunker and onto the battlefield. Darkness and then the terrible sound of explosions and war cries followed. When the noise stopped, the curtain fell, and slowly rose again revealing the muddy boots of the cast, lined up across the stage in military formation, still dressed in combat fatigues and helmets. They stood ghostlike and immovable in the smoke and haze, against the backdrop of a printed page, taken from a roster of British troops killed in the war. Thunderous applause from the audience was followed by the shuffling of playgoers exiting the theater in complete silence. What a production! The play is moving to Broadway later this year and will be re-cast with Americans. See it if you can. It is well worth the time and money.

After the play, we found another great French restaurant and visited with Katarina and Andrea over dinner. The two sisters had immigrated to the UK from Eastern Europe after their native Czechoslovakia split in 2009 along ethnic lines into the Czech Republic and Slovakia. Katarina and Andrea were Slovaks who found themselves in a newly formed country with limited opportunity and promise.

They began sharing a flat in London after Andrea completed her seminary education and was hired at Bloomsbury Church in pastoral counseling and visitation. Andrea, the more reserved of the sisters, had been instrumental in introducing Robert to the Bloomsbury parishioners and in involving him in some of the pastoral duties that he was eager to experience. Katarina, who also worked part time at the church, covering the front desk, entertained us with her backstage impressions of some of the more staid and traditional members of the congregation, as well as her candid views on several aspects of the politics of the church. I learned that some church issues are universal, and that the competing views of the older and younger generations on how the church will remain relevant in today's society is one of them. The conversation was lighthearted and fun, a welcome contrast to the visceral experience of war and conflict to which we had been exposed while attending the three-hour play. The evening was one of the highlights of our trip. Unfortunately, we forgot to take any pictures and thus this narrative will have to replace the photos.

Sunday, August 7. Sunday was Robert's last day at Bloomsbury Central Baptist Church, where he spent his summer break from Wake Divinity School volunteering his time conducting various pastoral and administrative tasks, and filling in for vacationing staff. Harry and I enjoyed attending the morning worship service and meeting some of the people with whom Robert had developed relationships over the summer. We chuckled over the way the British worded things as we read in the bulletin: *Welcome to Bob Stillerman's mother and brother, who have come to Bloomsbury to collect Bob.*

The church is located in London's West End, sandwiched between an affluent neighborhood and the historic impoverished area that was the setting for Charles Dickens' novels. Doors are open from 8:00—4:00 every day to the poor and homeless, as well as individuals and businesses from the play district wishing to use the facilities for auditions, play practice, and other community related meetings. Coffee, tea, and snacks are always available. The outreach from the vestibule is a major undertaking, requiring a full time facilities manager and numerous volunteers to staff the welcome desk. It is a tangible sign of Bloomsbury's commitment to an outreach of inclusiveness in the community.

The church maintains an active web page at *Bloomsbury.org*, where many excellent pictures of the sanctuary and inside facilities are posted, along with current information about the various ministries going on there. Robert posted pictures and descriptions about the church as well on his blog, *adeamondeaconinlondon.blogspot.com*.

Monday, August 8. Early Monday morning, we departed for Edinburgh. I booked first class seats to assure that we would be able to enjoy our four-hour trip in comfort and relative quiet. It was well worth the expense, as we were served a full English breakfast and lots of almost decent coffee (Even Starbucks can mess up a cup of coffee in the UK!), drinks, and gourmet sandwiches for lunch. It was reminiscent of railway trips I made as a child on the *Southerner* when we were served in the dining car from real china, linens, and silverware. The scenery became more and more exotic as we made our way north of London and the views of steep pastures dotted with sheep and cascading down to a rocky shoreline were breath taking.

Once in Edinburgh, we quickly settled in at the Princes Street Apartments, located just minutes from Waverly Train Station and the Royal Mile. On both Monday and Tuesday, the weather was absolutely perfect—sunny and a cool 65-70 degrees, and we walked our legs off exploring the Old Town and the surrounding sights, ending with the Military Tattoo on Tuesday night at dusk.

Wednesday, August 10. Wednesday, we awoke to a dreary sky and pouring rain. We had made reservations with Scotland Tours to take an eight-hour drive into the Highlands in a sixteen-passenger van, to see Loch Ness and other sights along the way. Colin, our tour guide, met us promptly at 8:00 am, at the bus stop just yards from the entrance to our apartment. Dressed in kilt, hiking boots, and a polo shirt, he entertained us with an endless store of trivia, stories, and anecdotes from the moment he pulled out of Princes Street until he returned us, tired and waterlogged, to our door that evening around 7:00 pm.

As we headed out of Edinburgh, Colin explained that there are two major areas of Scotland, the Lowlands, that we were currently leaving, and the Highlands. The

Highlanders were historically a spirited, independent, fierce, unafraid group of people, who owed their loyalty to their clan. Competing clans sometimes came to blows over land and cattle, and their battles were swift and brutal, often lasting less than half an hour. Many of the Highlanders were Jacobites, who opposed the reign of Protestant Mary and William of Orange (1688) and favored the return to the throne of the Stuarts under James II (of Scotland and VII of England). The Campbell clan proved an exception in that they were Protestant supporters of William and Mary, which put them at odds with the McDonalds, who were Catholic and loyal to the Stuarts.

The Highlands were so remote and wild that the inhabitants developed a code of hospitality that required any Highlander to extend food and lodging to any traveler who showed up at the door, even if the traveler were an enemy. One night, a group of travelers from the Campbell clan appeared at the home of a McDonald. The McDonald family took them in and gave the Campbells, their archenemies, food and housing for two weeks. At the end of the two weeks, the Cambells violated the code and slaughtered their hosts in their beds, thus becoming the most hated clan in the Highlands.

If the Highlanders were individualistic, independent, and fierce, the Lowlanders, according to

Colin, tended to be conventional, educated, well-to-do, and in touch with the fashions and trends of society. One of the most famous of Lowlanders was William Wallace, leader and martyr in the wars for Scottish independence in the thirteen hundreds. His statue guards the entrance of Edinburgh Castle, flanked by Robert the Bruce, warrior and first king of independent Scotland. Most Americans remember him from the movie *Braveheart*, where Mel Gibson, in the role of Wallace, raised his sword to lead the charge for *Fraaaaydom.*

Colin touted the movie, which he credits with popularizing the Highlands and bringing untold numbers of tourists to Scotland. However, he pointed out a major inaccuracy in the costuming. Wallace was a Lowlander and would never have painted his face, worn a kilt, and behaved as a Highlander. "You have to understand," he continued, "that most people think of Scotland as kilts and bagpipes. But that's only the Highlands."

Thursday, August 11. We left Edinburgh in the rain, early Thursday morning, and were delayed by an hour getting back to London due to flooding on the tracks. The trains in the UK have a reputation for running on time and you would have thought that we had been delayed by days rather than minutes judging from the frequency with which the engineer came on the intercom to apologize for the inconvenience.

Before checking into our hotel in Kensington, we stopped by Bloomsbury to pick up some baggage that we had stored in Andrea's office to lighten our load on the Scotland trip. John, one of the volunteers at the desk, updated us on the status of the riots that had broken out on August 6, in Tottenham, a northeastern neighborhood in London, after a peaceful protest of the death by police of a local man, Mark Duggan. While we were away, the looting and burning had spread in copycat fashion to other locations in London as well as the neighboring cities of Birmingham, Liverpool, Nottingham, and Bristol. The police appeared to have been taken off guard at the magnitude and random nature of the violence, and they were indecisive and slow in putting a stop to it.

Prime Minister David Cameron and other MP's cut short their vacations and returned to London to deal with the crisis. Tube stops near rioting neighborhoods were temporarily closed and the football match between England and Holland at Wembley was cancelled. John said that on his street, the merchants removed merchandise from the display windows and boarded up their shops to prevent vandalism and looting by the bands of disgruntled youths that were roaming neighborhoods and recklessly destroying property and striking out at innocent bystanders.

By Thursday, August 11, when we returned to London, the crisis had abated and everything appeared to be under control. The neighborhoods had been calm and without incident for several nights, due to increased police presence. Scotland Yard had identified murder suspects and over a thousand people had been arrested in connection with the violence, looting, and robbery. The House of Commons was engaged in spirited debate on long-term solutions for addressing the social issues underlying the violence. Bill Bratton, former New York and LA police chief, had been called in to consult with British law enforcement on gang violence and social unrest, a decision which gained mixed reviews and a few raised eyebrows from the British press.

Most of the news coverage we managed to find while in Edinburgh centered on the need for swift justice and accountability for the perpetrators of the senseless attacks on the innocent, as well as the looting, and destruction of property. Interviews of law officials, clergy, social workers, politicians, as well as citizens on the street denounced the violence as unacceptable acts of thuggery and brutality by bands of youth, undisciplined and out of control. They called for increased security and protection across the city, and favored a zero tolerance approach, with severe consequences imposed on any individual involved in action resulting in the destruction of lives or property.

At the same time, there was a discernible sense of recognition among those interviewed, as well as from the coverage on the debates from the floor of the Commons, that the implementation of a *Get Tough on Crime* approach could never address the root cause of the problem, which appears to reside in the anger of a youthful underclass, unemployed and ineligible for university, with nothing but time on their hands to act out their frustration and disillusionment. They seemed to concur that while looting and burning can never be tolerated by civilized society, neither can the repression and deprivation of basic human needs be ignored in the process of protecting the resources of the privileged while ignoring the plight of the underprivileged.

In the midst of our sightseeing and fun, twenty-five hundred miles away from home, came the jolting reminder of the widening gap that exists in our world between *Haves* and *Have-Nots*, which has been accentuated by a weak global economy, war, and natural disaster.

Competing with the story of the London riots that week, was the news of Standard and Poor's downgrade of the US credit rating from AAA to AA-plus, sending the stock market into a tailspin. Headlines across the UK read *US Humbled* and news analysts talked endlessly about what this might mean for the US economy and how this would affect the outcome of upcoming political contests between Democrats and Republicans. Would Sarah Palin or Michelle Bachman succeed in ousting Mr. Obama?

It was not the ideal time to be travelling, in terms of dollar-to-pound exchange rate, and the news about the US economy was beginning to give me nightmares about what the trip would ultimately cost. I was reassured when I called home to touch base with Bill. He put everything in perspective for me with his classic response to my financial jitters: "Don't worry," he said. "It's only money."

Kevin Spacey and Richard III

I have always been a fan of Kevin Spacey, and the minute I discovered that he would be performing in Shakespeare's *Richard III* at the Old Vic Theater during our stay in London, I ordered tickets for us to attend. I was so glad I did, because it turned out to be one of the hottest plays in London this summer and was completely sold out by the time we got there.

As our tickets were for the Thursday night, August 11 production, we checked into the Kensington Hotel on our return to London from Edinburgh, and freshened up for an evening at the theater. The Old Vic is located on the South Bank of the river, two blocks from Waterloo Station and the nearby Waterloo campus of Kings College, which houses the Florence Nightingale School of Nursing and Midwifery and parts of the Schools of Biomedicine and Dentistry.

Allowing extra time for sightseeing along the way, we left early and caught the Tube to the Embankment so that we could cross the Waterloo Bridge to the South Bank on foot and take in a few more of the sights across the river before the play. By walking, we misjudged the distance to the Old Vic and became a bit disoriented. Several times, as we paused to study the map and figure out our next steps, a friendly passerby would stop and ask if we were lost and needed directions, assuring us that we were on the right course and would run into the Old Vic a little farther down the street. These friendly gestures of neighborliness were a welcome surprise and went a long way toward calming and reassuring our anxiety about being out-and-about in the wake of the riots. We finally located the Old Vic, picked up our tickets, and still had time to grab a bite to eat before the production.

The play was well worth the effort and one of the highlights of the trip. Kevin Spacey gives a convincing performance as *Richard III*, who seeks by any means to eliminate all of his contenders to the throne of England, including his two nephews and a brother, standing in his way. He is cast as a modern day dictator, akin to Muammar Gaddafi or Hosni Mubarak in his ruthless quest for power, and to the likes of Zimbabwe's Robert Mugabe and North Korea's Kim Jong-il, in his paranoia and dysfunctional personality unleashed on their unfortunate subjects.

Spacey, the consummate villain, delivers his Shakespearean lines naturally and flawlessly, without British accent. For three hours and fifteen minutes, he is all over the stage, posture deformed by the weight of the hump on his back, toting a crutch, and strapped into a leg brace supporting his withered, pronated foot. Through every inch of the performance, from the opening *Now is the winter of our discontent...*to the near closing lines in which he cries, *A horse, A horse! My kingdom for a horse!* he pours his energy into the role, as he connects with the audience and makes them co-conspirators of his nasty deeds and Machiavellian plots, revealing a multi-faceted personality that is simultaneously evil, remorseful, cruel, charming, manic, and funny.

Spacey maintains this momentum to the end, when Richmond's forces have won the battle of Bosworth Field,

Richard is dead, and we see his lifeless body suspended by its heels from a rope and dangling above the battlefield, while Richmond is proclaimed victor and King of England, ultimately reining as Henry VII. Spacey hangs there motionless for a full two minutes as the play draws to conclusion.

An interview with Kevin Spacey printed in the program, quotes him as saying that the play is *a physically and emotionally demanding role, one that requires dexterity with language, and commitment to giving 150%. That's why I've stopped drinking, smoking, everything, to dedicate myself to this character.* No wonder!

August 12-14. Harry flew out early Saturday morning, leaving Robert and me a little bit envious that we were not going home with him. Robert was especially eager to get back after being gone for three months, and I was worn down by the pace we were keeping. However, we decided to hang in there and give it our best shot for the last three days.

Robert was anxious for me to meet Margaret and Keith, the couple he roomed with for the second half of the summer in their flat near the Tower of London, as well as to touch base with them and thank them for their hospitality. They were staying at their summer home at

Stratford-Upon-Avon and had asked us to come out and have lunch with them while we were traveling.

We decided go there on Sunday, August 13, and turned out making a full day of it. The train took us to Birmingham, where we had to navigate our way across town from New Street Station to Moor Station to catch a connecting train. We noticed a strong police presence as we de-boarded, and guessed it was due to the earlier rioting that had broken out in the city.

As we made our way toward Moor Station, which was on the opposite end of the commercial district called *the Bullring*, we felt a bit unsure of ourselves and quickened our pace as we tried to take in the sites and snap a few pictures along the way. At the only fork along the route, we went right when we should have gone left, and added about thirty minutes to our walk. We finally made the connection and arrived at Stratford-upon-Avon, which is a quaint, picturesque Elizabethan village that gives one the feeling of travelling back four hundred years in time.

We shared a delightful lunch with Margaret and Keith, at Carluccio's, their favorite Italian restaurant located on the Avon River, in the shadow of the Shakespeare Theater and Holy Trinity Church where Shakespeare is buried. Keith works for the government and is in charge of the public charging stations for electrical cars that are a part of a large grant to reduce oil dependency and provide alternative energy sources in the UK. Margaret is a retired educator who enjoys cooking and entertaining, and volunteering at the church. Both of them are longtime and devoted members of Bloomsbury Baptist Church, which they talked about with pride and great enthusiasm. They also appeared to be extremely devoted to Robert, which immediately increased their stock with me.

After lunch and farewells, Robert and I walked around the village before we headed back to catch the 5:00 pm train to London, chiding ourselves all the way that we did not get pictures with Margaret and Keith before we said our goodbyes.

The trip back was much easier than the one going over. We caught the express train this time and made the connection from Moor to New Street Station in less than ten minutes. On the ride out of Birmingham, we sat across from three young men who were in a party mood. One was dressed as Elvis Pressly, one as Pancho Villa, and the other was not wearing a discernible costume, but was so full of himself that he did not need to.

I stifled my curiosity as long as I could, and finally asked Pancho Villa why they were celebrating. He explained that they had just been to a cricket match where England had beaten India to become the winners in what might be the equivalent of our World Series in baseball. I congratulated them but was still confused about the significance of the Pancho Villa and Elvis costumes. Were these mascots or something of the like?

"Oh, no," he replied. "It's just a part of the festivity to dress up for these matches." I settled back in my seat, and closed my eyes, exhausted from the day's travel. Surrounded by the camaraderie and happy noise of fans rejoicing over their victory, I felt the warmth of familiarity and security. Except for the fact that I was twenty-five hundred miles from home, I could easily have opened my eyes to find myself in the midst of a bunch of Braves or Panther fans celebrating a win. Cricket, baseball, football, whatever the sport: team spirit is universal.

We ended the day with dinner at a nice British restaurant, recommended by the concierge at the hotel. Robert had invited our nephew Chip's brother-in-law John to join us, and it was wonderful to see him again and to talk with someone connected to family and home. John, an attorney with Wells Fargo, had arrived about the same time Robert arrived at Bloomsbury, to work on a six-month project in the company's London office before returning to his home base in Charlotte. We were chatting about the recent events in London and he told us about an eerie experience he had the previous week, while we were in Scotland.

John's attention had been consumed by the process of getting settled in his new surroundings, and he had not followed the news about the riots in detail. One night, he worked extra late before he took the Tube back to his flat, which is above a restaurant across town from his office in the business district. He was surprised to find that several of the Tube stops were temporarily closed due to nearby disturbances, in addition to those closed in preparation for the upcoming London Olympics, and he had to take a detour from his usual route, which was still somewhat new to him. As he crossed from the station into his neighborhood that was normally brightly lit and teeming with nightlife, he found the streets deserted and the storefronts dark and abandoned. He hurried on to his flat and was relieved when he got there safely and without incident. Later, he found out that the merchants had taken everything out of their display windows and shut their places of business down before dark, as a precaution against the looting and vandalism that had taken place in other neighborhoods. It was a similar story to the one we heard from John, the volunteer at Bloomsbury several days earlier.

In addition to our trip to Stratford-upon-Avon, Robert and I spent our last few days in London taking in the neighborhood around the Kensington Hotel where we were staying, and revisiting a few sites of particular interest to us. We enjoyed wandering around Hyde Park and then through Kensington Gardens, one of several enormous public parks in the area. It was fun to watch the families playing and relaxing together on the lawns—the adults sprawled out on blankets and the kids running around them with boundless energy, not unlike a scene from home.

We took a quick tour of the grounds around Kensington Palace and decided to go inside after discovering a sunken garden, decorated with hundreds of shiny orange orbs of varying sizes. This turned out to be a project left over from the IN TRANSIT Arts Festival that had been on the grounds in July. It was conceived as an interactive activity for the public, in coordination with the Enchanted Palace exhibit, which is also an interactive, tactile experience for the public, who, as they tour the palace, must find a set of clues in each of the rooms, revealing the secrets of the seven princesses who lived at Kensington throughout its history.

After completing the Enchanted Princess tour, visitors at the Arts Festival were invited to write their own secrets on paper and fold them inside the glass balls, to be hung throughout the sunken garden. They were left there for future visitors to enjoy and read. I thought how fragile the glass balls were, and was impressed that they had been entrusted to public hands. Just as I opened one and unfolded the paper revealing the secret, there came from behind me the sound of a bulb cracking like an egg on the gravel pathway.

I turned just in time to see an embarrassed elderly gentleman drop a folded paper on top of the shards of broken orange glass that were lying on the ground, and duck sheepishly out of the garden. Secretly relieved that my globe was not the one that had fallen, I replaced it carefully, and did not open any more of them.

Finding John Bunyan

Tuesday, August 13. Throughout our trip, we had been on the lookout for a statue of John Bunyan but had been unable to locate one. Bunyan (1628-1688), a Baptist forefather, is one of Bill's heroes for his stand on individual freedom as well as for the impact of *Pilgrim's Progress* on his (Bill's) thinking as a young seminarian introduced to the work for the first time, and the influence the book continued to have throughout his years as a pastor in the local church.

Robert did a *Google* search and found that the major statue of Bunyan is in Bedford, near his birthplace at Elstow and the crossroads where he first began to preach. He is buried in London, in the cemetery of Bunhill Fields, in the Burough of Islington, north of the City of London, next to three other historically famous nonconformists: George Fox (1624-1691), Daniel Defoe (1659-1731), and William Blake (1757-1827). Both locations were too far away to visit in the time allotted. However, we discovered that there was a rather impressive statue located back over near Bloomsbury Church in the Holborn area, where Bunyan actually died, and we set out to find it.

Bunyan became ill in 1628, after he had ridden out from Bedford to London to mediate a conflict between a father and son over an inheritance issue. He found himself too weak to return home, and took refuge with a friend named John Strudwick, who lived in Holborn. He died there at Strudwick's house, away from his wife and family.

The statue is in a niche on the front of the old headquarters of the Baptist Union, built in 1901. The headquarters has since relocated to Oxfordshire and the building is no longer in use. John Bunyan is holding a copy of *Pilgrim's Progress.* The sculptor is Richard Garbe, a late twentieth century artist influenced by the Victorian and Edwardian eras. The work is dated 1953, but it is thought that this may be an error, and instead should be 1903, as the sculpture resembles the artist's earlier works that are more decidedly Victorian than his later work that were art deco. In addition, the sculpture is located near two others of Edward I and Edward VII, both done by Garbe in his early years and similar in style.[2]

Back to Where We Started

Our last stop before leaving London for the hotel near Gatwick Airport, where we would spend the night, in order to make an early flight home on Tuesday, August 16, was back at the British Museum where we started our sightseeing tour on the first day.

Robert had visited the museum several times and recorded much of what he saw in his blog. I, on the other hand, had been jet-lagged and tired from the flight over, and had difficulty taking in very much of the vast treasures that are stored there. On our first visit there, I did see the Rosetta Stone, but most of our time was spent walking around in the Great Court under its spectacular glass and steel dome. The dome is an architectural work of art in itself. Designed to cover Europe's largest public square (two acres), it allows the sun to stream through its latticed surfaces, casting interesting geometric shadows on the white limestone walls and stairs of the Reading Room, where Karl Marx wrote *Das Kapital*, and creating an atmosphere of warmth and light throughout court.

We wandered around quite a bit among the Greek exhibit, and then took some pictures of the Egyptian exhibit for granddaughter Mattie, who got fired up about the pyramids and the Pharohs from studying about them in Bible School. The artifacts from the ancient world in this museum are overwhelming. Many were brought back during the height of British domination, when it is said that the sun never set on the British Empire. There is so much of the ancient world collected and housed here that one has to wonder if there is anything of antiquity left to see in Greece or Egypt. It was like the World Showcase at Epcot for the ancient world.

Home at Last

Wednesday, August 14. Although jet lag and the horrible exchange rate between the dollar and the pound left me depleted both physically and financially, the notion of a *next trip* was already stirring. My limited travel experience has confirmed two things: The extraordinary beauty of our planet and the strong cord that binds me to others who inhabit its surface now and in times gone by.

This insight came to me as I was standing on top of Edinburgh Castle, looking out over the medieval city built on volcanic rock, cascading down to the buildings of the Georgian New Town and continuing on out to the shore of the Firth of Forth, framed by mountains reminiscent of the Blue Ridge. I was overcome by the realization that our planet is truly a gorgeous, magnificent home. I resolved then and there to take advantage of every opportunity to travel and to see and experience more of it

As we explored the city of London on our night of arrival, wandering through Piccadilly Circus and pausing at Trafalgar Square to mingle with the crowd to take in the breathless views of the Thames and of Big Ben and Parliament rising into the evening sky, gilded by the rays of the setting sun; as we visited the Tower of London and the Globe Theater next day and tried to imagine the total devastation of the fire of 1666 on an already overcrowded city; as we snapped pictures of the statue of a dying Thomas a Becket in the gardens of St. Paul's Cathedral and overheard a British mother helping her son make sense of the event by explaining that the "the king was very cross with his best friend and had him killed"; I was stirred by the connection that I felt to all humanity both present and past who had visited those sites for the first time as I was doing, and experienced the wonder and excitement of discovery that I felt in those moments.

All that being said, I was equally excited when Robert and I boarded United Airways Flight 733, bound for Charlotte on August 15. Touching down safely at Charlotte Douglas International after a nine-hour flight, we hurried to get our baggage, find our car in long-term parking, and head up I-77 to Winston-Salem. When we finally crossed the Yadkin River, passed by Clemmons, and spotted the Silas Creek exit, I remembered that there really is no place like home.

On the weekend after returning from London, we celebrated a major milestone, our son Todd's fortieth birthday, at a big neighborhood barbeque in Charlotte, on Todd and wife Debbie's front lawn. We finished out the month with a trip to Atlanta for Grandmother Margies's annual birthday party, where all the Stillerman children, grandchildren, and great grandchildren gathered to celebrate and commemorate her ninety-two years.

A Family Memory

My first month of retirement ended with a trip to Georgia to celebrate Grandmother Margie's birthday. The party, an annual event for the family, had for the last decade been hosted by Bill's younger brother Jim and his wife Pam, at their spacious home in Social Circle, a bedroom community of Atlanta. The journey was long, and it was tempting to forgo driving down for the short overnight stay. However, it is always well worth the effort to be present at the gathering of the Stillerman clan to honor Grandmother Margie on her special day, which in 2011 marked her ninety-second year.

By blood and by marriage, our family roots run deep and have been nourished by fertile soil that feeds us and makes us strong. As our family tree continues to grow and branch out, separating us by distance and by responsibilities, the annual birthday party calls us back to our roots to renew the ties that bind, through the sharing of our favorite dishes and retelling of our favorite stories.

As always, the food and drink were sumptuous and plentiful. Outside, in the ample back yard, the guests sipped on fruity sangria, beer, and soft drinks around the pool, as we waited for Jim and Pam's famous Low County Boil to be served, steaming hot and spilled out onto a picnic table lined with newspaper. Inside in the cool kitchen, the granite counter groaned with side dishes prepared by each family member, and a giant platter of Covington's best, and probably the world's best, fried chicken.

There was something for every palette and taste, and everyone loaded up a plate with his or her favorite combination. For me, the *piece de resistance* was once again Pam's great aunt's old-fashioned eight-layered caramel cake, with icing so thick and sweet that I had to dilute it with a large scoop of homemade peach ice cream and wash it down with plenty of Chardonnay, so as not to lapse into to a glycemic coma.

As the scorching August sun began to disappear in the west, cooling things off a bit, the younger cousins stayed outside, to run barefoot and play in the yard, thrilled to be together and out of range of their parents' watchful eyes. The adults settled down inside, where we visited over second helpings of dessert, with coffee, and listened to the four Stillerman siblings joke and spar with one another about growing up in Atlanta.

As eldest son, David led off with the story about the time that his mother threw twelve boxes of Krispy Kreme Donuts down the basement stairs at their house on Peyton Road. He and younger brother Bill both played in the West End Elementary School Band and were required to sell donuts to raise money for their yearly trip to Daytona for the big band competition.

Their mother Margie had already bought dozens of boxes and had filled the freezer in the basement to capacity with the donuts that they had not eaten, sold, or given away. At that point, she put her foot down and clearly instructed the boys not to bring home any more donuts.

However, the band director was persuasive if not intimidating. At the next band session, he called on David and asked, "How many boxes can you sell this week?" David said, "Six." He continued down the roll, calling on Bill with the same question. Bill responded, "Six." When Margie spotted the two boys making their way through the kitchen door loaded down with twelve more boxes of Krispy Kremes, she completely lost it! She snatched up the boxes of donuts, threw open the basement door, and began hurling them down the steps.

The joking and sparring continued, as Bill engaged Jim in their ongoing argument about which of them was the least bald. David made fun of both his brothers and flaunted his full head of hair.

Their sister Jane told the story about the annual family Christmas Eve celebration around the tree and the year that Jim tried to read Luke: 2. The family custom initiated by their father Hy and mother Margie, was that, as soon as they were old enough, each of the children would be required to put on some kind of performance before they were allowed to open any presents. David would play his trumpet; Bill would play his clarinet; and,

Jane would play the piano. The year that Jim came of age, he chose to read the Christmas story from Luke: 2.

When this chubby little cherub with thick, horn-rimmed glasses, opened the family Bible and began to read, David and Bill *got their tickle boxes turned over*. Both parents shot stern glances at the two older boys and attempted to shush them as they dissolved into laughter. In the process, Hy got tickled, and before it was all over, everyone in the room but Jim was hysterical. From that year on, the reading of the Christmas story took on a new meaning and the mere mention of Luke:2 associated with Jim's name evoked a round of laughter and the retelling of the story.

As the adult conversation ran its course and the darkness came on, the children were rounded up from outside, and everyone gathered around the birthday cake for a rousing chorus of *Happy Birthday to You*, followed by the snapping of lots of pictures of the birthday girl blowing out the candles, with lots of help from the great-grandchildren. Grandmother Margie, as ever, was fully up to the occasion, looking radiant and soaking up the love and the energy surrounding her.

As the hour grew late, we reluctantly began gathering up our empty dishes and our children and grandchildren, and making our goodbye rounds. Happy and satiated with good food and loving company, we lingered to embrace each another one last time and to wish each other safe travel, before we scattered and returned to our separate lives.

We filed through the front door to hug and thank Jim and Pam for allowing us to invade and overrun their beautiful home, and made our way onto the front lawn and through the thicket of tall pines encircled by the haze, emanating from the warm summer earth as it rose to meet the cooling night air. High above, beaming down through the fog, the stars from a crystal-clear Georgia sky illuminated the path to the car-lined driveway where we claimed our rides and drove away from another joyous gathering of the Stillerman clan. Little did we know that in only a few short months, we would come together once again, returning to the arms of the family, to embrace one another in grief and loss.

The devastating news came in December that David had been diagnosed with Kidney cancer. After a valiant attempt by his medical team to treat the tumor with surgery and medication, David suffered complications resulting in a blood clot to the brain. On January 4, he died peacefully, surrounded by his wife Carol and his children.

As the family gathered, this time to celebrate David's life and mourn his loss, I thought about that happy night in August when we were all so recently together. I have filed it among my treasured memories, as a snapshot of the way we were.

CHAPTER 2

Resolution:

Control My Possessions (Before they Get Control of Me)

My trip to the UK was a wonderful diversion, as well as a giant step in fulfilling my resolution to travel to faraway places. However, it came so closely on the heels of my August 1 retirement date that I had not fully processed how I would incorporate my Retirement Project into my daily schedule and routine. An entire month had passed, and I realized that it was time to get to work. Controlling my possessions would be a good place to start.

Beginning in Earnest

The secret of getting ahead is getting started. The secret to getting started is breaking your complex overwhelming tasks into small manageable tasks and then starting on the first one. Mark Twain

Summer shouted its last hurrah in Winston-Salem with the passing of Labor Day. The kids were back in school; the Wake Forest football season was underway; and, the new television sitcoms and reality shows would soon be airing. Although the days were still humid and hot as blazes, the slight chill in the morning air and the shortening daylight hours betrayed the coming of fall. The signs were unmistakable. The inevitable change of seasons, both in the earth and in my life, had officially begun. There was no going back now. The hour had come to begin in earnest the daily business of living my vision for retirement.

On the first morning of the workweek following Labor Day weekend, I rose at 6:00 am, dressed in my workout clothes, and pulled up the Monday night edition of the David Letterman Show on the DVR in the living room. While Bill showered and dressed for work, I went through my exercise routine, relying on Letterman's monologue and guest lineup to distract me from the tedium of jogging in place and completing ten reps each of a set of floor exercises.

As Dave said goodnight to the audience, I finished my workout, clicked off the television, and headed to the kitchen. After pouring myself a cup of black coffee, I sat down at the bar to read the *Winston-Salem Journal* and complete the *Word Jumble*, which was becoming a part of my new daily ritual. I was still wearing my exercise shorts and my favorite yellow Paula Deen tee shirt with *Butter my Buns and Call me a Biscuit* written on the front. Even after thirty days of retirement, it felt a bit surreal at this hour not to be bathed, dressed, and heading down I-40 West to East Iredell Middle School. I could not deny the force of conditioning in compelling me back to the daily schedule that I had followed for thirty years, and I had to remind myself once again that familiarity of routine is not a valid reason to continue it.

At 7:00 am, Bill came through the kitchen to gather up his laptop and mobile phone, and to pour one last cup of coffee for the road. He bent down to hug me goodbye and headed out the door to his car to begin another twelve-hour day as the busy CEO of Baptist Retirement Homes of NC, Inc.

In the silence that surrounded me after his departure, I was confronted with a sense of aloneness and the extent to which I would be on my own in this new venture. Bill could not have been more supportive in encouraging me to pursue my retirement plans; but, as we peered together into our future, we were seeing through different lenses when it came to our respective careers and what lay on the horizon. In terms of our work lives, we were simply at different places in our journey. I knew from the start that I would be traveling this stretch of the road alone. To avoid indulging in a pity party, I pulled myself together, poured another cup of coffee, and began making a list of what I would do next.

One of my resolutions was to gain control of my possessions before they gained control of me. It made sense to start with a task that I could finish in a relatively short period of time, the completion of which would provide a quick dose of instant gratification to bolster my feeling of accomplishment and maintain motivation. Controlling my possessions seemed to be a good place to start

My first project was to sort through all of the *stuff* that Bill and I had collected in our forty-four years of marriage. We had become inundated and were suffocating under a mountain of possessions: book cases crammed with neglected and unread volumes; closets bulging with clothes I intended to wear when I lost ten pounds; kitchen cabinets bursting with multiple sets of china; a cupboard full of serving dishes and platters that could never be put to use, but were kept for sentimental reasons; and, stacks of unopened boxes filling the attic and basement, that had been gathering dust and haunting us with their contents ever since they were unloaded from the moving van that brought us to Winston Salem in 1986.

The recent experience of dragging twenty-five extra pounds of non-essential baggage across the UK for twelve days had become both a literal and metaphorical lesson on the folly of traveling through life overburdened by material things. The overstuffed suitcase that I had hauled around was a microcosm of my home, and for that matter, my entire existence. I determined as I began this journey into the next phase of my life that I would jettison all baggage, both physical and spiritual, that was weighing me down and hindering me from experiencing joy and fulfillment in the elder season. I was ready to start work on the physical baggage; the spiritual baggage would take a bit more time and reflection.

Armed with Peter Walsh's book *It's All too Much*, I proceeded, room by room, to clean and organize each space, and remove all clutter that had built up there. Walsh, an Australian-born expert on organizational design, has become a counselor to the millions of people in our country, from *hard-core hoarders* to *clutter victims* suffering from an epidemic of over-accumulation in a culture of super-consumerism. He is convinced that most Americans display at least minor symptoms of this condition and his diagnosis for all of us who are afflicted is simple and to the point: *You are no longer controlling your stuff. Your stuff is controlling you.*[1]

Chapter by chapter, step by step in *It's All Too Much,* Walsh outlines a remedy that he guarantees will enable even the most persistent of the hard-core hoarders to gain control of their *stuff* and consequently their lives. As one who was more of a clutterer than a hoarder, I was especially optimistic about my chances of recovery, and I was ready to dig right in and get started on the regimen. The results were overwhelming. By the end of September, I had made astounding progress in clearing away the clutter and getting our house back in order. At the risk of engaging in too much tedium and detail, I will not recount every step of the process but instead will share only a few insights from the book that especially helped me in de-cluttering and simplifying my world.

Walsh explains that as our possessions pile up and we accumulate more than we can possibly use, we become like pack rats, cramming things into any available space to make room for them. Outgrown clothes that will not fit into the closet go to the basement; unused sports equipment that will not fit into the garage goes in the coat closet; and magazines and bills that we refuse to throw away are deposited on counters and the tops of drawers. As a result, rooms lose their functionality, a clear sign that the house and the people in it are suffering from overload. When overload occurs, it means that our things are now controlling us rather than us controlling our things, as it should be.

That leads to one of Walsh's cardinal rules: *Every room in the house must serve its own unique function.* Once that function is determined, anything in the room that does not contribute should be removed and stored in another place. For example, a bedroom is for sleep and relaxation and getting dressed. It should be set up as a peaceful, quiet place where the light can be shut out, and where the clothes are organized and easy to access, rather than thrown over a chair or piled on the bed.

If a room must serve more than one purpose, it should be organized into areas according to purpose. For example, a den can function as a playroom for the children and a craft center for hobbies, as well as place for the family to watch television together. For that to be successful, the room should be organized into distinct zones, with the toys confined to one space, the craft items organized in another, and the television, easy chairs, and DVD's grouped together. Walsh warns that it is difficult to keep a room clutter free if it serves too many functions.[2]

Implementing this rule in our house helped me see the purpose of bringing order to the random manner in which I had been storing everything from family memorabilia to outdated software manuals and extra writing materials. During past bouts of spring-cleaning, I had dusted and straightened, and even disposed of some of the clutter. However, I had always put things back on those same shelves in the same random order. In the kitchen alone, bills were stored next to the first aid kit; batteries and tools sat next to old CD's and bottle of Wild Turkey that we used to spike the eggnog at Christmas; a jar of pennies served as a bookend for old cookbooks, and on and on it went. Our home began to take on a pleasing new sense of order as I cleaned, sorted, and separated items according to purpose, and then found places to store them together or at least in close proximity.

A corollary to this rule is that the function of each room should be determined in advance of any major clean-up effort, after family discussion and input. Bill and I had no problem in reaching consensus on almost every area of the house. The garage, on the other hand, is the bane of Bill's existence, and keeps piling up with things that I want to get out of the house and things that the children have left there and never claimed. It all sits, gathering dust and crowding out the tools and yard equipment that would reasonably be stored there. I know that we will figure out some way to deal with it eventually, but probably not in the immediate future.

Another of Walsh's rules of particular relevance to my situation is that people must learn to live within the space they currently have in their homes in the same way they must learn to live within their income. The excuse of saving things because we might move into a bigger home or add on to the existing one, does not hold water with Walsh, who contends that we must deal with our clutter and gain control of it in the present. If not, then, even in the event that we do one day have extra room, we will simply fill that space to the brim and be back to where we started.

Walsh is clear about how all of this works, if we really want to control our possessions rather than have them control us. For example, when it comes to books, we can keep only as many as our shelves will hold. It is a matter of physics. If the shelf holds two hundred books, then that is how many we can keep. No excuses! The rest will need to be sold or given away.

He soundly debunks the claim that we are holding onto books because we may someday want to read or re-read them, by arguing that the likelihood that we will do that is very slim. Even if that time comes, it is cheaper to access the book online or buy another copy than to have it occupying precious space needed for the volumes that we treasure and frequently read and enjoy.

The same principle applies when it comes to clothes. There is no way to fit fifty dresses into three feet of hanging space or to store fifty tee shirts in one hundred cubic feet of drawer space. Only those items that will fit comfortably into the closet and drawers should be kept. All of the clothes in our closets and drawers that remain should be ones that fit, that we like, and that we wear on a regular basis. Anything else should be sold, given away, or trashed.

Walsh suggests that we try the Reverse Clothes Hanger trick that will prove his eighty/twenty rule that we wear twenty percent of our clothes eighty percent of the time, and to help us decide what should go and what should stay. We are to turn all of the clothes hanging in our closets so that the hangers face back to front. For the next six months, every time an item is worn, we are to replace it on the hanger, turning it back the correct way. After six months, we are to look to see which clothes are still turned in the wrong direction. Those are the ones that we need to give away. I did not need to try this exercise to be convinced that Walsh is right. One look in my closet provided object lesson enough for me.

I am doing a much better job now of living within my space, but books and clothes continue to be a challenge that I have not completely mastered. Even more of a challenge was Walsh's rule that you only keep the family pictures and heirlooms that you really like and can display and use. It may seem heartless, he concurs, to get rid of grandma's old china, when it was so special to her; but, if it is crammed in the back of the cupboard, collecting dust and taking up space, it cannot be that important to you or to her memory.

Walsh reminds us that our memories of our departed loved ones do not reside in the possessions that were once theirs, but in our minds and hearts. Besides, if we truly intended to honor an individual with an item that has been handed down to us, we would make a proper place for it, display it, or bring it out and use it from time to time. As hard as it was for me to accept, I took that suggestion to heart as I began pulling out all of the china and silver and stemware that had come to us as wedding gifts, or that had belonged to my grandmother or mother. I polished the silver and put it in tarnish-proof bags; I washed the china, threw out the chipped and broken pieces, and boxed it up in sets; and, I gathered up and cleaned all of the ornamental bowls and serving dishes, and sorted them by size and category.

I forced myself to choose one set of china, one set of stemware, one of each type of serving dish or ornamental bowl, and only the pieces of silver that I would be willing to commit to keeping polished and on display. All of those items were returned to the shelves and cupboard and the rest I offered to the children. What the children did not take, I gave away to friends or to charity. Now, I revel in the space that was once filled with clutter.

The possessions that I did retain mean all the more to me because there is ample room now to display them and enjoy them. Almost daily, I pass through my dining room and admire the handsome silver candlesticks and silver serving platter displayed on the buffet, that Bill and I received as wedding gifts. I think of my mother and how she would smile to find that her Wedgewood Audubon bird plates and the crystal stemware that she picked out before she and my daddy were married, are decorating my hutch. I remember my little German grandmother as I trace my fingertip over the gold leaf letters printed on her decorative china canisters now placed on the shelf beneath the bird plates, and try to decipher the meaning of their German labels of *Graupen, Reis, and Delkin.*

By the end of September, I had sorted through and de-cluttered every room in the house and Bill had loaded up the boxes and bags I had marked for disposal and driven them to their various destinations, which included the dump, the Habitat Re-Store, Goodwill, Salvation Army, and the Rescue Mission. Together, we had moved a mountain of stuff. It felt good to get out from under the load. The garage still stands as an exception.

Eating the Elephant One Bite at a Time

The next project was one that I dreaded, because of the huge amount of physical and emotional energy it would require. I am referring to the mountain of my dad's stuff that was crammed into a storage unit over on Country Club Road at Colonial Storage. We have been paying monthly rent on the space for three years now, since my sister Betsy and I dismantled Daddy's apartment at The Gardens of Taylor Glen to move him into assisted living, at ninety-one, after his health began to decline.

There was only room enough in assisted living for Daddy's bed, his clothes, and a few of his personal items. Therefore, we gathered up and gave away boxes of things to which we had no personal attachment and the rest went either with Betsy to her home in Garner or to me in Winston Salem, i.e., the storage unit. We had been through this process seven years earlier when Daddy dismantled his house in Wake Forest and downsized into an independent living apartment at Taylor Glen, in Concord, North Carolina.

Daddy died in December, shortly after his ninety-second birthday, and his stuff was just sitting over there haunting me, not to mention costing us a sizeable amount to maintain in its current dusty and disorganized state. As frugal as Daddy was, he was no doubt stirring in his grave over my extravagance. It would not be the first time.

On several occasions, I had ventured over to begin the process of culling through it all; but I would always panic at the sight.

There were cartons full of

Bills,

Cancelled checks

Tax returns and forms

Medical records

Investment reports

Loan agreements

Insurance forms

Passports

Birth certificates

Marriage and death certificates

Military records

Awards and plaques, and an

Inventory of household goods,

All meticulously organized and packaged and labeled, paper-clipped and rubber-banded together

There were cardboard boxes filled with

Sermons

My dad's lesson notes

Theology books

Paper and office supplies

A kit for making a mandolin

Puzzles

Framed pictures

Mirrors

My mother's china, silverware, stem ware, bowls, and

Various and sundry pieces of memorabilia collected over a lifetime

And crowded among the stacks of boxes were

Lamps and shades

A Gott water cooler

Daddy's golf shoes, tennis racket and tennis balls

Daddy's seminary office desk and chair

File cabinet

Captain's chair

Roller cart

My mother's secretary desk

Embroidered footstool

Stepladder

Two card tables

A padded bedstead, and

Grandmother Poerschke's bedroom suite—bed, mattress, chest of drawers, vanity

The list reads like that Shel Silverstein poem *Sarah Cynthia Sylvia Stout who would not take the Garbage out*. Except, it was not garbage. It was the remaining artifacts of my parents' lives. Gradually, I realized that my panic at dealing with their things rose out of unresolved grief over my father's death and the fear of being confronted with the pain as I stirred up the dust of memories that lay among my father and my mother's randomly assembled possessions in that storage closet.

Each new attempt to begin the process had ended within minutes after I lifted the door and surveyed the boxes. The panic would rise and I would shake my head, throw up my hands, and get out of there as quickly as it took to lock up the unit and punch in the exit code to open the gate to the premises.

The last year of my father's life had not been his best. He had remained active and mentally alert well past his ninetieth birthday, when he managed to renew his North Carolina Driver's License, to the surprise and concern of everyone in the family. However, as his health began to decline in his ninety-first year, he chafed under the growing limitations to energy and movement imposed by his aging body and exacerbated by an earlier fall which had left him with a broken femur from which he never fully recovered. He deeply resented the loss of independence suffered when forced by the early onset of dementia to move into assisted living and surrender his driver's license. He never fully adjusted to the new regimen in assisted living; and, as his dementia advanced, he drew further into himself and became progressively more confused and agitated, often experiencing hallucinatory dreams, so vivid that he could not distinguish them from reality.

The person he became stood in stark contrast to my formerly vigorous, energetic father, who had maintained the dexterity to water ski around the lake at seventy-five, and whose mind was still sharp enough in his eighties to explore how quantum physics and New Age Theology could be incorporated into his existing belief system. He retained his handsome looks—full head of hair turned white, and pale blue, piercing Poerschke eyes. Even in his nineties, his physique was still impressive—broad shoulders, long legs, sturdy frame.

A *forty-ish* doctor was examining him in the emergency room during one of his many trips to the hospital while he was at Taylor Glen. After reviewing his chart, she exclaimed, "This says you are ninety years old. You are beautiful!"

She pulled back the sheet, exposing him in his hospital gown. "Look at those legs. They are to die for. And that face! You must have been drop-dead gorgeous when you were younger." And he was, and continued to be handsome, smart, athletic, confident, and stubbornly independent. In body and mind, he had defied age for so long that we thought he could do it forever. My sister and I joked more than once that he would probably outlive us both. That is why it was so difficult to accept his inevitable decline.

My immediate response to his death on December 3, 2010, was one of relief and gratitude that he did not have to linger in his current state. The images of his final days and months served to numb my sense of loss for a while. Almost a year passed before the reality set in that the last of my two surviving parents, and a major fixture in my life, was gone. I had grieved thoroughly for my mother, when she died of ovarian cancer in 1992, still in the prime of life. I learned from that experience how the chronic ache of loss gradually gives way to feelings of joy and gratitude for the rich memories that remain. In the case of my dad's death, that process was still incomplete.

I was simply not ready to uncover the treasure of memories that lay in those boxes of my parents' possessions that had become my responsibility. I felt like Sarah Cynthia Sylvia Stout, the custodian of a big container of *garbage piled up so high it reached the sky*. I feared that if I did not do something with it before it *got too late*, I might suffer the fate of poor Sarah, who was buried under the mound of trash, all because she did not heed her father's warning to *Always take the garbage out*.[3]

Thank God for Shred-It

Time passed and with it came new perspective, as well as an urgency to clear out the storage unit so that we could stop paying rent on it. Spurred by my recent success with the house, I decided to return to the unit and begin anew. Almost immediately, after I pulled up the door, my panic returned and quickly began to rise along with my blood pressure. As I searched for a reason not to bolt once again, I remembered the old joke: *How do you eat an elephant? Well, one bite at a time, of course.* I took a deep breath and decided to follow the advice from the punch line of that joke.

My first *bite* was to take a quick survey of the boxes and attach a yellow sticky note on every box that I was sure could be trashed or shredded in its entirety. It took about an hour to complete the task, and when I was finished, I had identified nineteen boxes matching that criterion.

As I pulled down the metal door and secured the lock to the storage unit, I began planning the next step, which would be to get Bill to help me stack all of the boxes with sticky notes together to get them ready for shredding. The removal of nineteen boxes would be a critical step in freeing up space to organize all of the remaining things.

Once at home, I *Googled* shredding companies and discovered one in our area that would make house calls. I made immediate contact with Suzette, at Shred-It, who assured me that all I had to do was call her by Friday and she would have the truck come to the door of the storage unit on any given Tuesday. The *shred monster* would destroy about a box a minute, paper clips and all. It would even eat small three ring binders.

I got on the schedule for the next Tuesday, and at the appointed time, I met the driver at the gate of the storage company, and directed him to the unit. In less than thirty minutes, he had hoisted all nineteen boxes up into his truck and fed them into the jaws of the giant shredder, paper clips, metal binders, staples and all. I thanked the driver and gladly handed him a check for his services. It was money well spent. With the boxes gone, about thirty percent of space was freed up, and it was easy to see what needed to be done next. The ten-or-so boxes that were left, contained books, notes, china, and a variety of personal treasures. Now that I had de-cluttered the house, there was room to move them home and sort through them there.

Back in the car, I continued planning, as I entered the security code on the pad to activate the gate, and drove home. The next *bite* I determined would be to identify the pieces of furniture, lamps, and pictures that we or the children wanted to keep and the things that we wanted to give away, and begin taking them to the Habitat Re-store or another charity.

With a ton of effort on Bill's part, and with help from Shred-It, I have eaten that elephant bite by bite, until all that remains in the once crowded storage room is empty space.

CHAPTER 3
Resolution: *Write to Publish*

If you wish to be a writer, write. Epictetus

By October, I was blogging regularly as a part of my resolution to write and publish. I was also working on several other projects as I sought to develop my voice as a writer and to experiment with various mediums and genre. I am including a few of the later blogs in this chapter, along with descriptions and excerpts from the projects. The blogs can be viewed in entirety at amostretired@blogspot.com.(Note that the web address contains a typo. *Almost* should be entered as *amost*.)

Meeting Fred Chappell
(October 17, 2011 blog)

I had the opportunity on a Sunday afternoon in October to go with Harry to hear Fred Chappell, one of my favorite Southern writers, who was reading from and discussing his works, at Mitchell College. The public library sponsored this event as a part of the *Iredell Reads* project, which focused for the month of October on Chappell's novel *I am One of You Forever*.

I am One of You was the first in Chappell's tetralogy of coming of age novels, published in 1985. *Brighten the Corner Where You Are* was published in 1989, followed by *Farewell I'm Bound to Leave You* in 1996, and *Look Back all the Green Valley,* in 1999.

After being introduced to his writing in *I am One of You Forever* over a decade ago, I read the other three of Chappell's coming of age novels, one by one, as soon as they came off the press. I was intrigued not only with the author's telling of his story about growing up in the forties on a farm in the mountains around Canton, NC, but also with his ability to weave the language of poetry into his prose, as well as mix realistic narrative with the telling of tall tales and yarns and mountain lore. You do not have to read very far to understand that Chappell is one of the region's gifted writers, ranking in the same league with authors such as Lee Smith and Clyde Edgerton and Ferrell Sams. His long tenure as a member of the English Department at UNCG before his retirement, allows the Triad to claim him as one of our most treasured local gems, as he is still living in the Greensboro area.

Chappell read from *I am One of You* a large portion of the first chapter entitled *The Good Time*, in which he introduces Johnson Gibbs, the young hired hand from the orphanage, who the Kirkman family take into their home, come to love as a son and brother, and ultimately must grieve when he is tragically killed in a training accident at Fort Bragg. In Chappell's own voice that retains a hint of mountain twang even after years in the Piedmont, he set up the relationship between Johnson and Jess's father Joe Robert, which foreshadows the impending tragedy of Johnson's death:

"'There ain't nothing better than this," Johnson said.

"From here it is all downhill." He sat up and hugged his knees.

"I'll bet the best time is over for me after this."[1]

The chapter entitled *The Telegram* is the one about Johnson's death and the way the family all accepted the news and the loss in his/her own individual ways. It is one of the saddest, but most poignant and beautifully written accounts of bad news and its aftermath that I have ever read. Chappell talked about how it came to be but did not want to read it aloud because it was so sad.

Chappell was a boy of eight or nine at the height of World War II, when people were receiving news every day of battle casualties. He was walking down the street in his home town of Canton and saw a small house up on the hill with black curtains and all the shades drawn. Only in the front window, the shade was raised enough to reveal two gold stars placed side by side in a display case. Chappell said that he was too young to understand what it all meant but that the scene evoked in him a sadness and melancholy that defied words; and, it was one that he will never forget. It was this feeling that he wanted to convey in the chapter about Johnson Gibb's death.

The telegram ... *sat on the dining table propped against the blue-and-white ringed sugar bowl... glowed yellow like an ugly pus,* and would not go away until each member of the family had completed the agonizing ritual of making peace in his/her own way with Johnson's death.[2] It was a powerful, universal symbol---that dreaded telegram—connecting the story of the Kirkmans' loss of Johnson Gibbs with the story of countless families in past and present as they are forced to read the words and confront the chilling fact that the latest casualty of war was one of their own.

At times, Chappell's writing moves from realistic narrative to telling tall tales, as was the case in several of the chapters about the visiting uncles—*Uncle Luden the Rover, Uncle Gurton and the Beard, Uncle Zeno and the Unfinished Stories,* and *Uncle Runkin and the Coffin.* Someone in the audience asked Chappell if he really did have any relatives like the eccentric uncles who visited in the story, and he replied, "Yeah, don't you?"

"But was what you wrote about them all true?" the audience member persisted. Chappell told her, with a sly grin and a twinkle in his eye, that what he wrote was not always fact, but it was always true. He said that as a writer, it is sometimes difficult to remember every detail of the way things are, and so the imagination fills in and the story becomes a mixture of what you actually remember and what you filled in. He considers the product of memory and imagination to be true if not always factual.

Another audience member asked whether Chappell preferred writing poetry or prose, as he has been so successful with both. Chappell has published numerous books of poetry along with his fiction, serving as North Carolina's Poet Laureate from 1997-2002. Chappell said he prefers to write poetry and thinks of himself primarily as a poet, although he has been successful as a prose writer. However, he cautions his students about trying to do both. "Just pick one or the other and stick with that," he recommends.

The reason he gave was that poetry is like a snapshot of life, fixed in time. It is intense and demands an economy of carefully chosen words to produce the desired effect; whereas, prose takes place over time and can be developed through the telling of a story, with dialogue, and through extended details.

As a final question, someone asked what literature has influenced him and who are some of the young up-and-coming writers he is following. Chappell said that he has read *Don Quixote* eight times and that as a young man he was intrigued with *The Sun Also Rises,* but he thinks that he was drawn to the latter work then because in his early years he loved to fish and do outdoor things, as well as drink and raise hell.

Chappell confessed that when he retired he had planned to read all of the books he was supposed to have read and claimed to have read when he was younger. However, he has found that he is barraged with manuscripts from former students and aspiring local writers who want him to read and comment on their work, leaving him time to read little else. Their writing is prolific and of good quality, and Chappell says that this is the up-and-coming work he is watching.

Fred Chappell is a celebrated writer and a local gem. He admits to being a bit shy, and is extremely down to earth and approachable despite his success. He is obviously a teacher at heart, who is willing to share his experiences and to promote and encourage others to hone their writing skills. He began the session by reading a few of the poems collected from a local writing group of older adults. I will remember his kindness in autographing everyone's copy of *I am One of You* and for asking me if I were Kathy with a *K* or Kathy with a *C* before he signed my copy, as well as complimenting me on my sweater with the pretty roses.

All in all, it was an afternoon well spent, listening to a celebrated writer talk about his craft. Thank you, Harry, for inviting me.

Seek the Truth No Matter Where You Find It (October 2, 2011 blog)

Last year, for the first time ever, I surprised myself and developed a personal mission statement. It is short and sweet and to the point; but I will probably spend the rest of my life growing into it.

To Live Purposefully
To Love Unconditionally
To Learn Perpetually
To Laugh Frequently

My motivation to complete this task came from attending a three-day training with my entire staff on the *Seven Habits of Highly Effective People*. I know. I have always been dismissive of the *Seven Habits* as simplistic and commercialized. To be honest, my reaction to the story that Stephen Covey tells about chastising a father for not controlling his unruly children on the bus, only to learn that they are on their way home from the hospital after their mother has just died, is one of cynicism. Nevertheless, amid the trappings of melodrama and sentimentality and commercialism, I also found in the *Seven Habits of Highly Effective People* profound principles that have helped me to focus on managing this bold new adventure called retirement that I have recently undertaken.

I struggled mightily to accept this revelation. As an old liberal skeptic, I have always had a tendency to write off any idea or theory that comes with a sales pitch and smacks of sentimentality. I like for my insights to be pithy, to spring from authentic, intrinsically motivated sources, especially those associated with my own political and philosophical worldview. Basically, I like to find my truth from the pulpits of open-minded churches, the Democratic Party, the great Southern storytellers, and the liberal media. You could call me narrow-mindedly liberal and snobbishly inclusive.

One of my dad's core beliefs was John 8:32—*And ye shall know the truth and the truth shall make you free.* A corollary to this belief, and one that was just as important to him, was that *you had better be ready to accept truth wherever you find it, because it will not always show up where you expect it or want it to be*. My dad was much more esoteric and erudite than I. For him, that led to exploring how the truths of New Age Theology and physics could be incorporated into his belief system. He sought new truths about the laws of the universe and the cosmos. I am still trying to figure out how to live and grow with purpose on this planet.

That may be why the *Seven Habits* had a particularly truthful ring for me. As Stephen Covey himself explains, the habits are based on timeless and universal principles that govern how we grow successfully from dependence to independence to interdependence. He did not invent them. He was just smart enough to name them, package them, and market them to millions of eager consumers.

I admit it. I would have preferred to gain my insight from a different source. But, there I was in August of 2010, standing in front of sixty-five disgruntled staff members whom I had coerced into returning to school three days early. There I was, welcoming them back to school and introducing them to the Franklin Covey facilitator who would teach us how to use the *Seven Habits* to help us work together to promote a culture of leadership among ourselves and our students. There, in the midst of my low expectations and the even lower expectations of my staff, we found some convincing truths that would inform not only our personal lives but also our collective lives as a community of educators seeking to ignite a passion for learning in our students and ourselves.

Our facilitator, Lonnie Moore, an author and former middle school teacher, was engaging and funny, and had us all eating out of his hand by the end of the first day, with anecdotes about his attempt to implement a leadership culture in his own classroom by teaching and modeling the *Seven Habits* for his students. I came away from the workshop with some very valuable tools for successful living, not the least of which was *To Begin with the End in Mind* by creating a personal mission statement. The habit of beginning with the end in mind is the habit of vision. It enables us to live by design rather than by default. I like the quote from *Alice's Adventures in Wonderland* printed in the Covey manual:

Would you tell me please which way I ought to go from here?
That depends a good deal on where you want to get to, said the Cat.
I don't much care where, said Alice.

Then it doesn't much matter which way you go,
said the Cat.[3]

That is how I became motivated to write a personal mission statement and how I found truth in a place that I did not expect it to be.

The Nonnie Project

For years, I have been working on a collection of stories about my grandmother, Martha Bryant Kendrick. She was affectionately called Mattie B. or *Mattee* by the grownups, but all the grandchildren, or *Grands* as she referred to us, called her *Nonnie.* I am hoping eventually to publish the completed memoir, written from the perspective of her *First Grand,* as a means of introducing her posthumously to all of her great-grand and great-great grandchildren. I am sure that if the likes of all of them could ever get together, they would hit it off, and there would be a party so lively it would wake the neighbors.

My stories of Nonnie are all drawn from her maturing years, as she aged into the spirited and determined woman who learned to drive, bought a car, and acquired her driver's license at seventy-six; who held down a full time job until she turned seventy-eight; and who played the piano for Sunday services at the juvenile detention center and entertained the *poor old souls* at the local nursing homes with her melodica, well into her mid-eighties, when she was gradually robbed of her vitality, as her mind was taken over with dementia. The Nonnie I remembered was like a colorful character in a southern novel, not unlike Mattie Rigsby in Clyde Edgerton's *Walking Across Egypt* or Tolitha in Pat Conroy's *Prince of Tides*. In fact, I fantasized that one day, I might be able to develop my own novel, loosely based on her life

Though I had my own rich collection of memories of her later life, which were embellished by stories and anecdotes from my mother and uncle and cousins, I knew very little of the rather unique and even tragic circumstances of her years as a young woman. Nevertheless, I was intrigued by those circumstances and suspected that they had played a huge role in shaping and defining the independent and self-sufficient woman that she became. I had pieced together the bare outlines of her story from the sketchy details that I learned from my mother and from Nonnie herself, who rarely spoke of that time in her life.

Nonnie graduated from Normal school at the Greenville Female Academy in Greenville, South Carolina, in 1906, at the age of eighteen. Her first teaching position was in the neighboring town of Taylors, where she boarded in the home of John Kendrick, a wealthy banker, and his wife Cora. In 1911, while she was still living with the Kendricks, John's wife died suddenly and left behind four sons, the youngest of whom was two. Mr. Kendrick, who was eighteen years her senior, turned to my grandmother for comfort and for support with the children. They were married in 1912, at the First Baptist Church in Greenville.

My uncle Schaefer was born in 1916, and my mother was born eight years later, in 1924. In 1929, John Kendrick lost all of his holdings in the stock market crash and suffered a mental breakdown from which he never recovered. He was in and out of the State mental hospital in Columbia, and died there in 1935.

He was never again able to care for his family, either financially or emotionally, forcing my grandmother to leave their home and move to Greenville to seek employment that would provide her with sufficient resources to support her three minor children. She never remarried and lived out the remainder of her life relying on her own resourcefulness, the guidance of the Almighty, and the love and support of her children and her family.

Since my retirement, I have devoted significant time to the Nonnie project and have even shared some of my first drafts with my cousin Beth and my sister Betsy. It is still very much a work in progress; however, I am committed to see it through to some type of publication by the end of my second year of retirement.

I have included below an excerpt from the material.

In Memory of Mattie B.

At first, the disease came on her like a petty thief, snatching inconsequential memories and causing a mild forgetfulness: the name on the tip of the tongue that could not be recovered, the pot that became scorched from being left on the stove too long, the missed appointment. It was nothing to become alarmed about; just one of those annoyances of aging.

In time, however, the thief grew bolder, making off with large chunks of her memory, robbing her of her personality, and rendering her unrecognizable to those who knew and loved her. Back then, they called it *a hardening of the arteries*. Now, the diagnosis would be Alzheimer's or some type of dementia. By whatever name, it had its way with her and by the end, had transformed my grandmother into a wild-eyed and confused, addled and restless stranger.

Physically, she had not changed much. She still maintained her trim form, erect posture, and girl-like figure. Years of healthy living and exercise had paid off.

Even when she was well into her into her eighties, her family physician would tell her that she had the body of a sixty year old. However, the memory loss dimmed the light that had formerly danced in the soft brown eyes. The melodic sound that emanated from her vocal cords when she would throw back her head and laugh with her entire body ceased. Her mind simply wore out before her body did.

The memory loss was a harbinger of her increasing state of dementia and confusion. My cousin Beth recalls that they became convincingly aware of it the day she appeared at the top of the basement stairs in multiple sets of clothes. She had put on underwear, panty hose, a slip, a dress, shoes, and then started all over again.

It became evident to my mother and Uncle Schaefer that it would no longer be safe for Nonnie to live independently in her little garage apartment in Greenville. By that time, both my sister Betsy and I were grown and married, and there were three empty bedrooms at my parents' home. They packed up Nonnie's belongings and took her back to live with them in Wake Forest.

As the dementia progressed, she began to shuffle about with no purpose in her step, her movement and speech repetitive and redundant. Routinely, when I was visiting in my parents' home in Wake Forest I would observe her go to the wall phone in my mother's kitchen, pick up the receiver and repeat:

"Katherine, I think I'll call Schaefer."

"Okay, mother. Why don't you do that?'

Still holding the receiver and poised to dial...

"Katherine, I think I'll call Schaefer."

"Okay, mother."

Still holding the receiver with finger pointing aimlessly in the air...

"Katherine, I think I'll call Schaefer."

"Mother, he's not back from the office yet. Why don't you put down the phone and we'll

dial him later?"

Every night as my mother prepared dinner, Nonnie would wander into the kitchen and ask:

"Katherine, can I do anything to help?"

"Well, mother, you can set the table if you like."

Moving toward the utensil drawer...

"Katherine, I wish you'd let me help you."

"Okay, mother, you can get the silverware out of the drawer and set the table."

Rumbling in the silverware drawer ..

"Katherine, I declare. I really would like to help you."

"It's okay, mother. Dinner's almost ready. Why don't you go in the bathroom and freshen up?"

One morning, I brought our oldest son Todd, who was a toddler, over to stay with his grandmother Kat and great grandmother Nonnie while I went out to do some shopping. They all decided to go out for a walk and some fresh air. Mother and Daddy's house was on a sloping lot with a steep set of brick steps leading to the road.

Mother hauled the stroller up the steps and then went back to help Todd and Nonnie up. She got Todd situated in the stroller and gave him a banana to keep him entertained. She had to dash back in the house to get the keys and lock the door, and, she instructed Nonnie to keep her eye on Todd and said that she would be right back.

When she returned only moments later, she heard Todd crying, "Mine! Mine!" and Nonnie contradicting, "No, it's mine!" She glanced up just in time to see Nonnie trying to wrestle the banana from Todd's hands.

This stranger stood in stark contrast to the vibrant woman who had always moved gracefully and effortlessly among us. Before, she thrived on family gatherings, flitting from one relative to the other to hug and kiss and catch up on the news and gossip since the last event. She took a special interest in all of the children and could frequently be overheard exclaiming to a grandniece or nephew:

"Now, you come over here and give me a big hug, you precious thing. I've been so hungry to see you. Your mother says you're just the smartest child in Greenville, nearly."

Like many southern women of her era, Nonnie tended to take the Scarlett O'Hara approach to anything that was unpleasant or distasteful by dismissing it until later. She figured that if she ignored old age long enough, it would go away. And, I will have to say, it worked pretty well for her for a long time. She was almost seventy when she took me to Washington, D.C. for a week, and she walked me around to see so many sites that my twelve year-old tongue was hanging out by the end of each day.

Mattie B. was always up for a party and there was nothing that energized her like being among the people she loved. She dressed up and tried to look her best whenever she met her public, for one thing, she did not want to look was old. As she aged into her late seventies and early eighties, she maintained such a youthful appearance and zest for life that she always received compliments from the cousins who had not seen her for a while. "Aunt Mattie, you are amazing. You don't look a day over fifty. How old are you anyway?"

"Aw Pshaw," she would exclaim. "Nobody gives a hoot about how old I am," and she would change the subject.

Having graduated from college when she was eighteen, she was only sixty-eight when her fiftieth reunion at Furman rolled around. She conveniently arranged to be away from Greenville, planning a visit to our house in Siler City to coincide with the date. When my mother found out she had skipped the reunion, she asked her why in the world she did not go. Nonnie replied, "I didn't want to be around all those old people."

Knowing how much she enjoyed playing the piano, Schaefer gave her a melodica, a keyboard instrument about two octaves long that was activated by blowing through a mouthpiece. It was light and portable and she immediately began taking it with her to the local nursing homes to make music for all of those "poor old souls" out there. It never occurred to her that she was older than most of them.

Ultimately, Nonnie's demise came after she fell and broke her hip and was unable to regain mobility, even after six months of recuperation and therapy. Her condition deteriorated to the point that she was bed ridden and no longer recognized my mother or my uncle Schaefer. At that point, her children reluctantly decided to admit her to a skilled nursing facility in Greer. She continued to decline there and she died on a cold snowy day in January, 1975.

My mother and Nonnie's only daughter, was half a world away, in the Philippines, where she had gone with my dad who was on Sabbatical from Southeastern Seminary to teach for a semester at the Philippine Baptist Seminary at Baguio. My Uncle Schaefer was recuperating from a heart attack and had strict orders from his doctor to avoid undue stress. Under the circumstances, the family decided to hold a simple memorial service at the graveside in Springwood Cemetery in downtown Greenville.

We were living in Mount Gilead, where my husband Bill was serving as minister at the First Baptist Church, when we received the call from Schaefer that Nonnie had died. I was thirty-one and six-months pregnant with John, our second child, and still commuting to Wadesboro where I taught French and history part time at Southview Academy.

I remember feeling little emotion at hearing the news of her death; and, when Schaefer remarked that it was a blessing that she did not have to linger any longer, I agreed matter-of-factly.

In truth, her actual death marked the formal recognition of a phenomenon that had occurred several years prior; and, the immediate news evoked no sense of grief or loss. As Schaefer would say it more eloquently years later in one of his columns, *Tireless death had ridden yet another time for his purposes; but this time he was not the villain, he was the hero.* After I jotted down the details of the memorial service, Schaefer and I said our goodbyes. I organized some lesson plans for a substitute and began making arrangements for the trip to Greenville.[4]

Mother had confronted the likelihood that Nonnie might die before she returned from the Philippines and had concluded after much urging from the immediate family, that she would not come back for the funeral if that happened. It was a practical decision and really the only reasonable one, but one that she later admitted she shed bitter tears over when she received the news shortly after she arrived in Baguio, jet lagged, disoriented, and eight thousand miles from home.

Had all of that happened today, we could have e-mailed or Skyped each other and made instant contact. As it was in 1975, we had difficulty making even a phone connection and with the thirteen-hour time difference, it was a day or so after the funeral before I was able to talk to Mother. Even then, the connection was poor and there was an echo in the line that made it almost impossible to carry on a decent conversation.

On the day of the funeral, it was bitter cold. Bill and I left our house around 8:00 am and it sleeted and snowed all the way to Greenville. My mood was gray and reflective of the weather. I missed my mother and could not imagine that I was taking this journey to lay my grandmother to rest without Mother being there.

We made our way down I-85, bound for Greenville, Nonnie's home during all the years I had known her, as well as the center and gathering place for my mother's side of the family. Familiar sights and landmarks along the road that always signaled our progress toward the much-anticipated destination were obscured and rendered unrecognizable by the fog enveloping the landscape and the mixture of sleet and snow pelting the windshields and blurring our vision. The atmosphere in and outside the car was gloomy.

As we passed into Spartanburg County and drew nearer to Greenville, there was a slight lifting of the fog and the sky lightened. By the time we arrived at Springwood Cemetery and joined the small band of mourners at the gravesite, the snow had stopped and the sun had begun to peek through the clouds. Dr. LD Johnson, Nonnie's former pastor and close family friend, began his eulogy by saying: *Miss Mattie and I had a secret love affair*. By the time he completed his touching words about my grandmother, the clouds had parted, and the sun had returned in all of its splendor, shining down through a magnificent blue sky to warm the gathered crowd.

There, in the clear, crisp daylight, from the plot where Nonnie's remains were laid, all the familiar landmarks that held her memories surrounded her— Schaefer's old law office, the US Post Office building where she had worked for Congressman Bob Ashmore, the Old First Baptist Church where she was married, the park where she took us to visit the mangy buffalo, the Waffle Shop in the Poinsett Hotel that had been a regular stop for breakfast. Clearly visible on the horizon, the panorama of the Blue Ridge stretched out maternal arms to cradle the city and her resting place.

With the reading of the 121st Psalm that concluded the service, I could hear Nonnie's voice reciting the words *I will lift up mine eyes unto the hills...* The tears began to flow, followed by uncontrollable sobs. In that moment, the wild eyed-stranger released her grip upon my memory and I began to grieve for the vibrant woman who was my grandmother.

In due course the grief subsided and has been replaced by an overwhelming sense of gratitude for Nonnie and for the thirty-one years I was privileged to share with her as her *First Grand.*

As the years pass, the circle of those who knew and loved Nonnie has dwindled. I am now one among a few of the lone generation that survives to carry her memory. I feel a real sense of urgency to find the words that will capture her essence so that I can introduce her properly to her Great and Great-great Grands. Besides, there is that gnawing fear that if I wait too long to write things down, my own memory may succumb to the thief of Alzheimer's as did my grandmother and my great aunts Ressie and Annie Mae. The disease does tend to run in our family. Hopefully, I have dodged that gene or someone will discover a cure before it gets to me. In the meantime, I am going to get busy writing.

Church Characters

Church Characters is the working title for a set of fictional character sketches I have been writing, based on some of the colorful individuals who passed through our lives during the years that Bill served as pastor of local churches in the Piedmont and then in a small community twenty-five miles east of Raleigh. I have included two of the completed ones below.

BB

BB was a hypochondriac who was devoted to the mission work of the church, both at home and abroad. She regularly sent her offering to Lottie Moon at Christmas time and was active in her missionary circle, writing get well letters and visiting the sick and infirm in the congregation whenever she was not, herself, undergoing one of her numerous surgeries or treatments from one of her many specialists in Charlotte.

When Rev. P did his home visits and hospital rounds, she was, more often than not, on the list to be seen. On the occasions when she was well enough to attend the Sunday service, she would stop by the ladies' room before entering the sanctuary and corner some unwitting visitor waiting her turn in line. She would inquire about their wellbeing first, and then launch into an excruciatingly detailed and personal description of her most current malady.

One spring day, Rev. P and his family had strolled three blocks from the parsonage down to the Sundry Center for a bite of lunch. They were crowded into the back booth, where the oldest boys were finishing up hot dogs and orders of fries. The nine-month old twins were entertaining themselves with *dripless* ice cream cones that the waitress and owner had cleverly devised by pinching off the end of the cone and pushing a dab of vanilla ice cream far enough down into the broken cone to be sucked out of the bottom without making a mess. They were sucking away, enjoying their mess-free treat, when BB walked by their table on her way back from the ladies' room.

Spotting the reverend and his family, she drew closer to the table. Rev. P rose to his feet, wiping his mouth with his napkin and extending his hand to greet her.

"Well, good afternoon," she chirped. "I hope you are all enjoying a delightful lunch," and then bending down to pat the head of the oldest son who was the one nearest her reach, she made eye contact with him and said sweetly, "I just lost mine."

On another occasion, six weeks into her recovery from her second back surgery, she felt the urge to get out of the house and visit her mother, who was suffering from advanced stages of dementia and had been committed to a nursing facility in a nearby town. The mother had wandered out of the house in the middle of the night and almost got hit by a pulpwood truck as she made her way onto highway 70, barefooted and dressed only in her flannel night gown.

She knew that Rev. P paid regular visits to her mother and called the church office to inquire about the date of his next trip to ask if she could ride along. Rev. P was accustomed to using his travel time to practice his sermons, and he somewhat resented the intrusion, but he was gracious and told her that he would pick her up at her house at 11:00 o'clock on the following Tuesday.

When he arrived at her house, she informed him that she had consulted her physician who advised her that she was free to participate in any activity that involved standing or lying flat on her back, as long as she did not sit for more than ten minutes at a time. The trip to the nursing home would take about twenty minutes.

"So," she instructed. "If you'll just help me into your back seat, I'll ride flat on my back all the way, and I can just stand during my visit with mother." All the way to the nursing home and back, Rev. P was a captive audience to the constant sound of BB, rehearsing for him all of the experiences of her second back surgery, from beginning to gory end.

Reverend P. returned home late that afternoon and seriously considered breaking out the fifth of Jack Daniels, a Christmas gift from his brother. He settled instead for a couple of aspirin and a cup of coffee, when he remembered that he was scheduled to be at the church for a building committee meeting at 7:00.

DM

DM was Pale and wan, with dyed, black Minnie Mouse curls and thin lips made pouty with an excess of Revlon's darkest red. She suffered from malaise—a marriage gone bad and three hyperactive boys who would drive anybody to drink, plus a daughter who dressed like Elvira until she found Jesus and joined the Salvation Army Band.

With great feeling and enthusiasm, she regularly performed piano preludes and postludes for the Sunday worship service that almost, but not quite, masked the sounds of the Jones boys arguing and slugging it out on the second pew. Playing her music on Sunday was the best part of her life—one place she felt in control and in the spotlight.

She caressed the keys and the notes from *Chariots of Fire* wafted out over the sanctuary:

Ba rum' dee dum dum' dum'

Ba rum' dee dum dum'

Ba rum' dee dum dum' dum'

Dum' dum' dee dum' dum'

Reverend P, who had just finished having a word of prayer with his deacons before the service, sprang from his study in horror, mumbling to himself, "What in the hell kinda music does she think she is playing in church?" while members of the congregation whispered to each other, "Wasn't that just beautiful?"

At the end of each performance, she wore exhaustion and fatigue on her face like a badge. One Sunday, she was so fully into the role that she fainted on the front pew.

For a long time, no one noticed her, even though she was spread out like a diva performing her dying scene, limp hand draped across her face, playing to an absent audience.

Finally, someone collecting the bulletins left in the pews saw her lying there and suggested that she might need assistance. No one hurried to her side. It was hardly the response that DM expected and she let everybody know it.

Grandchildren

Family faces are magic mirrors. Looking at people who belong to us, we see the past, present, and future.

Gail Lumet Buckley

Although not much of a poet, I had been working for some time on a set of rhyming couplets about my six grandchildren. I wanted to explore the subject of the unique traits and idiosyncrasies that made them so adorable and irresistible, and to do so with a simplicity and subtlety of language that would not betray me as a sappy old grandmother besotted by her grandchildren. The economy of words that poetry requires appeared to make it the ideal genre to fit my purpose.

I finished the poems in November and began selecting photos of the children which were stored on the Shutterfly website (the photos, not the children) to match each one. Todd helped me set up the photos and text to create a 7x9 inch booklet, with a two-page spread featuring each child and his/her poem, along with pictures. Before and after each two-page feature, we added collages of group and family pictures. I ordered ten copies from Shutterfly to give to the children and Grandmother Margie at Christmas, and kept the remaining copies for myself. The poems follow.

Child of My Child: Heart of My Heart

It is hard to believe that there could be any creature more amazing than your own child. You live with that certainty for years, and then one day a grandchild comes along and deepens your understanding of what *amazing* really is. Your very own child is your heart. The child of your very own child is the heart of your heart. Watching him or her is watching your child again for the first time. What you see is so familiar and similar and yet so unique and new. The baby is like a prism, through which myriad family traits refract, bend, and reveal themselves— grandpa's chin, mama's eyes, daddy's furrowed brow, sister's fair complexion, brother's temper. The light shifts; the view is altered; the baby grows and changes and amazes.

These little rhymes reflect a tiny spec of what I see in the prisms that are my grandchildren, viewed through the eyes of a grandmother. Each continues to grow and change and yet each remains child of my child, heart of my heart.

CHARLOTTE RAE

When Charlotte Rae comes out to play, she wears a smile that spreads a mile
Across her face.

Charlotte Rae with eyes of blue and hair bow just a bit askew
Will melt your heart when she grins at you.

Charlotte has a button nose and likes to wiggle all her toes.

She thinks it is a special treat to kick her socks right off her feet.

Charlotte's patient, Charlotte's kind, but she will surely speak her mind
If Henry hugs a bit too tight or she wakes up hungry in the night.

Charlotte Rae is one big flirt. She bats her eyes and swishes her skirt,
And causes all the little boys to turn their heads and drop their toys.

Charlotte Rae will have some fun but she'll let you know when she is done.
After all, she's almost one.

ANDERSON THOMAS

Anderson, who just turned one, can crawl as fast as I can run.
His honey curls and eyes so bright will make you want to squeeze him tight.

But, you had better hold him fast and get some kisses while they last,
Before he's off across the floor, to find more places to explore.

Andy is a man of action. In his bare feet, he gets traction.
Up to lofty heights he goes, which keeps his mother on her toes.

Andy's busy as can be. He has no time to humor me.
But, I will steal a little hug, as he speeds by me on the rug.

Andy's calm and sweet and fair, with rosy cheeks and curly hair.
Come on in and take a peep. Little Andy is asleep.

JOHN WILSON

John Wilson, or Jack, as he is known, can talk to you like he is grown.
He'll point his finger and explain, in terms so clear and words so plain

With his dark brown eyes and furrowed brow, I forget for the moment, I don't know how,
That in spite of the way he speaks to me,
This little boy is only three.

Jack likes to help and he'll work hard at Daddy's side to mow the yard.
He shops with mother at the store, and likes to do most any chore.

He plays with his toys around the house, and watches Handy Manny and Mickey Mouse.
He hangs out with little brother Andy, and he loves Skittles and M and M candy.

Here's a secret you should know: Jack likes his serious side to show.
But, if you tickle him he'll giggle, laugh aloud, and start to wiggle.
That is when I'll steal my hug, from this little cuddle bug.

HENRY KENDRICK

Henry Kendrick could win a prize with his long thick lashes
and his big blue eyes.
He's three years old and smart as can be, and he always
has a hug for me.

Henry's learned his songs and stories by heart.
He can tell them to you from finish to start.

One's a Halloween tale with moans and groans,
And a part about *shake, shake, shakin' them bones.*

School is a place that Henry enjoys.
He likes to play with the girls and boys.

Amanda is his best *gril* friend
And he's faithful to her to the end.

But he's glad to come home at the end of the day
To Momma and Daddy and Charlotte Rae.

And when dinner is over and stories are read.
He'll cuddle up with *SchoolTeddy* and go to bed.

Henry is tender and he is kind, and even when he forgets
to mind
All you have to do is ask, and he will get right back on
task.

WILLIAM TODD, JR.

Will Stillerman will soon turn four; he's not a baby
anymore.
He's learned his letters and his numbers too. He can count
anything out for you.

Will is strong and he is fast! Watch him speed as he runs past
All the other kids of three, and four, and five, and six,
And me!

Will lights up whenever you play any song by Roger Day.
He'll sing out loud that *it's a no-no, for anyone to kiss a rhino.*
Will's a good sport and likes to play. He is happy to do things
Mattie's way.
But if his heart is just not in it, he'll tell you *No* in a Texas minute.

Will is sweet and he is shy. He'll duck his head
and cock his eye.
When he peers through tousled bangs at me,
 I hug him tight and wish he'd stay three.

MATTIE KATHERINE

Mattie Katherine has it made. She's just tuned seven and is in first grade.
She's good at soccer and choir and ballet, and does her homework every day.

She loves her teacher and her friends at school and tries to follow every rule.
She is learning to count and read and write, and studies about
Egypt and the stars in the night.

Mattie's heart is made of gold. She cares about others who are hungry and cold.
She walks for hunger and does all she can, to help the world and her fellow
(Wo)man.

Mattie knows how to act and dress like one of Disney's
Princesses.
She likes Snow White and Rapunzel and Belle,
But her all-time favorite is Ariel.

Mattie has green eyes that twinkle and glow, and a smile
so warm it could melt the
snow.
She's growing up, that's plain to see. But she'll always
have a hug for her E-Dad and me.

CHAPTER 4

Resolution: *Get Fit and Healthy*

The best six doctors anywhere
And no one can deny it
Are sunshine, water, rest, and air
Exercise and diet.
These six will gladly you attend
If only you are willing
Your mind they'll ease
Your will they'll mend
And charge you not a shilling.
Nursery rhyme quoted by Wayne Fields, *What the River Knows*, 1990

The Battle of the Bulge

For the most part, I was pleased with how my Retirement Project was progressing. My attempt to sift through all of the excess baggage and get down to the basics had paid off. I had de-cluttered most of the drawers and closets in our home and the place had taken on a definite order. Bill had remarked several times that he could not believe how nice it was to have the extra space and to find things in their places instead of having to rummage through piles of unrelated items to find a screw driver or a roll of tape or a flashlight. The rental space with Daddy's things was coming under control, and we were optimistic that it could soon be vacated completely.

I had consulted the timeline for my Retirement Project action plan and found that I was right on track with all of my goals. Aside from the cleaning and organizing, I was blogging on a regular basis, had completed a set of poems about my grandchildren, and was making good progress on a memoir of my grandmother that I had been working on for several years. I had also started attending a Sunday school class at Knollwood, as a first step in reversing my twenty-year status as a church drop out. Things were moving along quite well.

Like a first grader who just got a smiley face or a gold star from the teacher, I was feeling all proud and even a bit self-righteous about my accomplishments. And then, I ran smack dab into a brick wall. It is the same one I have been running into for years: my weight.

Regardless of what I do, I seem to reach a plateau above my ideal weight and then gain and lose the same two to three pounds over and over. My *Battle of the Bulge* has been ongoing for as long as I can remember. I have managed to win a number of skirmishes, but have never succeeded in permanently winning the war.

The first Monday in November, I had started on a new program of eating less and exercising more. On Friday, after four days of adhering strictly to the plan, I stepped on the scale in my bathroom, hoping for positive results. Once again, I was confronted with the dreaded two-pound gain instead of the three-pound loss I had hoped for. The numbers could easily have been reflecting a temporary water gain or the fact that my body was trying to adjust to the new regimen; but I did not persevere long enough to prove or disprove either theory. Instead, defeat dampened my mood and my resolve submerged under its weight. I made a quick trip to the stash of Halloween candy I was *only keeping around for the grandchildren* and helped myself to the rest of the miniature Twix bars.

Regret and self-reproach followed the mini candy binge as I bid goodbye to the prospect of getting back into my skinny clothes any time soon. (Peter Walsh's rules be damned! I was still hanging on to those.) I continued my pity party throughout the weekend to the point that Bill asked me several times if there was anything wrong. I said I just did not feel very well, and I actually was fighting a pretty bad chest cold.

But, the truth was, it was all about the yo-yo weight gain. Had the scale given me the news I wanted, I would have been energized and motivated, and ready to move mountains. As it was, I felt heavy and dull and unattractive; and, it was all over two little pounds. There is simply nothing that drags me down like gaining weight. So why in the world did I go on fighting the *Battle of the Bulge*? Why couldn't I figure out a way to win the war and be done with it?

By Monday, I had finished wallowing in self-pity, and was ready to pick myself up and begin again. I did the only thing I knew to do: make a new plan and try to follow it. I briefly considered doing something drastic to lose five quick pounds, like going on that dreadful cabbage soup diet for a week. However, I remembered that I was sick of it by the third day, and ended up with no pounds lost and a gallon of soup in the refrigerator. Besides, all of the diet research I have ever read clearly shows that successful weight loss results from life-long changes in eating rather than a sprint to drop a few pounds just to gain them back.

They say that people do not perform up to expectation for two basic reasons: either they cannot do it because they lack the skills or knowledge, or they will not do it because they lack the motivation and will I cannot plead guilty to lack of knowledge in failing to meet my weight loss goals. I have spent so many hours reading books and articles on diet and nutrition, in hopes of finding a quick fix to my weight problem, that I could have earned a degree in it. No, my failure to lose weight is not because I cannot do it. It is obviously, because I will not do it. Motivation or will, then, is what stands in the way.

I decided to begin again with the basics and build my new weight loss plan on proven principles of diet and nutrition. I made a list of *Diet Do's* and committed to the short-term goal of losing at least ten pounds, reducing my waist size to thirty-four inches, and getting my BMI down below twenty-seven.

<u>Diet Do's</u>

1. DO keep a food diary of everything I eat.

2. DO use a pedometer to track my exercise and walk at least 1200 steps per day.

3. DO reduce my food intake by at least 200 calories per day.

4. DO eliminate sugar.

5. DO eat lots of lean protein.

6. DO eat two servings of fruit per day.

7. DO eat at least three servings of vegetables a day.

8. DO eat small meals.

9. DO have planned snacks.

10.DO drink plenty of water.

I found a site similar to the Weight Watcher's web site, only it is free, that allowed me to track weight, record food intake, track exercise, and get support in the form of recipes and diet suggestions. There is also the option of posting progress on Facebook and signing up with a buddy. I decided to use that site to track my progress. I was not so sure about the buddy and the posting on Facebook, but left the possibility open for later.[1]

I was ready to begin my new lifestyle change when my chest cold became worse and I started feeling absolutely awful. I ended up going to the doctor for an antibiotic and remained under the weather for several days. Needless to say, that delayed my plans, as I am not one of those lucky ones to lose weight when sick. Instead, I tend to seek comfort food, which is usually heavy on dairy fat and empty carbs. My recovery took me into Thanksgiving weekend, which as anyone knows, is not the ideal time to start a new diet regimen.

I set Monday, November 28, as the official date for starting the plan that would ultimately lead to the end of a yo-yo dieting syndrome and a slimmer and healthier me. This time, I planned to win the battle of the bulge for good.

By January, I had made good progress. I had gotten through the Christmas holidays without losing ground and was almost ten pounds lighter than when I started on November 28. I was using the free website at *everydayhealth.com* to record my food intake and exercise, and I found that it kept me focused and on task most of the time.

For the next few months, there was little progress made and my weight began to yo-yo again. I would gain a pound and then lose it, and eventually gain two and only lose one. By June, I had re-gained almost five pounds, and I knew it was time for a new strategy. I decided to get some help from the Beverly Hills Weight Loss Center, where I had experienced some success in the past. The diet, low fat/no sugar/limited carbs, is similar to the one I was already following. It includes four high protein supplements taken throughout the day to stabilize the metabolism and prevent hunger. The counselors are professional and friendly, and the weekly weigh-ins serve to keep me accountable. By the end of July, I had lost about seven pounds, bringing the total loss to twelve pounds from when I started November 28, 2011. I am hopeful that by November 28 of 2012, I will have brought the total loss to at least twenty pounds, so that I can justify holding onto my skinny clothes despite Peter Walsh's advice to the contrary.

CHAPTER 5

Resolution:

Embrace Loss and Sorrow

One of my resolutions was to embrace the loss and sorrow in my life, both from the past and as I move into the future. I had begun that process in two areas that I had previously identified. The unresolved grief over my father's death had eased as I summoned the emotional energy to go through his things in the storage closet and to confront the memories that lay there. I had found as well that my sense of loss over ending a thirty-year career as an educator was subsiding, as I began to wake up to my new reality and engage in my new life.

However, I was completely caught off-guard by the sorrow, abruptly arriving at the beginning of the holiday season to jolt the entire Stillerman family, as rudely as a nightmare rouses a child from a peaceful sleep.

A Gift Unexpected

On December 10, the news about which I forewarned in the account of Grandmother Margie's birthday party rocked our family. David had been diagnosed with Kidney Cancer, with a tumor blocking the inferior vena cava.

Ironically, Bill and I were on our way down to Atlanta for an early Christmas celebration with his mom when we received the news. We were set to have dinner in Fayetteville with the brothers and sisters, and some of our favorite cousins, Roy and Fern, Uncle Harry's children, and Roy's wife Candee. The three of them had flown in from Plymouth, Massachusetts, and Richmond, Virginia, and were staying with Bill's sister Jane and her husband Jim in their home there in Fayeteville.

Jim Stillerman, David's physician as well as his brother, called just as we were leaving the house to inform us of the diagnosis and to suggest that we go directly to the hospital instead of his and Pam's house in Social Circle, where we had planned to spend the night as well as ride together to Fayetteville.

Jim told Bill that they would schedule surgery for David as soon as possible at Dekalb Medical Center in Atlanta. He was certain that the kidney would need to be removed and was extremely concerned about the tumor in the vein and the delicate nature of dealing with that without throwing a clot. At that time, he felt relatively confident that the cancer had not spread and was hoping that a few suspicious spots on the liver could be dealt with during surgery. Jim would fill us in on the details once David and his wife Carol met with the specialists later on in the morning.

Bill got off the phone and we hurried to get on our way. We rode in shocked silence almost to Charlotte, wanting to arrive there but dreading what in the world we would say to David and Carol. We were completely rocked by the news and could not imagine how much more devastated they must be. My cell phone rang and it was David himself, calling to let us know he was being released from the hospital, and directing us to go to Jim and Pam's house as formerly planned. He sounded strong and upbeat and, in that vintage take-charge David style, informed us that he had been cleared to go home and was planning on attending the dinner in Fayetteville that night.

We arrived in Social Circle in midafternoon at Jim and Pam's lovely home, all decorated out for the season and smelling of spices and Christmas goodies. Over cups of coffee brewed from their new Keurig, we visited and barraged Jim with questions about next steps for David's treatment as well as his mental outlook. Jim said that David had reacted practically and pragmatically. He simply wanted to know if the specialists could remove the kidney and get the tumor in the vein. When they answered affirmatively, he was ready to *get on with it* and *get the job done.*

David was not interested in hearing many specifics about the medical procedures. Meg, his older daughter, on the other hand, asked numerous questions and inquired about every detail of what the medical team would be doing for her dad. In the days to come, she created a Caring Bridge web site and faithfully posted updates about David's progress in clear, non-technical language. The postings were a real godsend to the family and the many friends who waited anxiously for news about his condition.

We were fearful about David trying to do too much on his release from the hospital, but Jim assured us that his going to the dinner posed little risk and would probably be good for him. As it turned out, it was a wonderfully therapeutic evening for all of us and just the kind of Christmas gift we all needed.

David and Carol joined us at Jim and Pam's house around 5:00 pm so that we could all go together down to Fayetteville. Despite the fact that her world had been turned upside down only hours earlier, Carol had baked an apple pie to take to the dinner. She was, as always, her sweet calm self, and instantly put us all at ease with her gracious, loving manner.

Bill and I offered to drive our car to keep from having to be too crowded, but Jim insisted that we all travel together. We were successful in squeezing all of the early Christmas presents that Bill and I had brought from North Carolina, Carol's pie and Pam's appetizer and vegetable dish, plus the seven of us into their spacious Cadillac SUV. Pam and son Tom, who had the dubious honor of being the only representative of the younger generation, volunteered to sit in the third seat, with Bill, Carol, and I in the middle, and David in front with Jim driving. It was the first time in years we had all been together without all of the kids and grandkids. We had such a good time all cuddled up together, cocooned in Jim and Pam's luxury car. We talked and laughed all the way from Covington to Fayetteville and it seemed like no time before the hour-long trip was over.

Jane, Jim, and Mom had prepared a delicious dinner of flank steak and twice baked potatoes, rolls, and salad with greens from their garden. Paired with Pam's fresh green beans and Carol's apple pie topped with ice cream, we enjoyed a perfect pre-Christmas meal. We all sat around the dining room table and reminisced about Christmases past and the good times our families had together when we would gather at Mom and Dad's home for the holiday season.

As always, Mom looked pretty and festive in her Christmas sweater, and was equal to the task of leading us in the traditional *Mushy Moments with Margie,* the name our nephew Chip had affectionately given to the family sharing time when each person was asked to tell a favorite Christmas memory. It was a special treat to have Roy, Candee, and Fern among us. For a few hours, time was suspended, and we all soaked up the love and fellowship that is always present when families take time to be together. Too soon, we would have to get back to reality and the difficult challenge ahead for David. But for a little while, we took respite in one another and drew strength from our joy in being together.

I will always appreciate that evening as a precious Christmas gift come early from David and Carol. The two of them had just been given crushing news earlier in the day. David was facing serious surgery and the fight of his life. Both of them had every reason to withdraw, shut the world out, and take time to deal with the news in private. Instead, they reacted with their typical faith and courage, gracing us all with their presence for dinner, and giving us all the opportunity to be with them and draw strength from them and from one another.

A Bittersweet Christmas

David's surgery took place on December 21. The surgeons were able to remove the kidney and spleen, but not the tumor from the vena cava, which had grown too far into the vein to take out without being life threatening. The biopsy on the spots from the liver indicated that the cancer had not spread. Although the news was not positive in terms of curing the cancer, the family was encouraged when they met with the oncologist, who outlined further treatment to contain the spreading of the tumor on the vena cava.

David improved rapidly from the surgery and was making excellent progress until December 24, when he threw a blood clot, causing him to aspirate into his lungs. His condition became critical and he was moved to ICU. Christmas Day came and went with little change in his condition. David remained in ICU, with Carol at his side. Hope was kept alive through the outpouring of love and support from their children, their family, and a multitude of friends who were in constant prayer for his recovery.

Christmas was a bittersweet season for the Stillerman family. Even so, we all experienced once again, perhaps this time more deeply and poignantly, the love and joy and peace of God come down to earth to be with us and to sustain us.

Sweeping Up the Heart

The Bustle in a House
The morning after Death
Is solemnest of industries
Enacted upon Earth—

The Sweeping up the Heart,
And putting Love Away
We shall not want to use again
Until Eternity [1]
Emily Dickenson

On January 3, David had a stroke from which he could not recover. He died peacefully and without pain on January 4, surrounded by his loving wife Carol and his children. Family and numerous friends memorialized him on January 7, at the First Presbyterian Church in Covington, Georgia.

David's passing left a huge hole in the lives of all our family. He was much too young and we lost him way too soon. Once again, we were reminded that life is fleeting and precious and we will do well in the relatively short time that it is ours to embrace it and all of those around us. David certainly did that, as evidenced by the outpouring of love and support on his behalf during his short illness and as he was memorialized

The process of *sweeping up of the heart and putting love away* is one we all face in our own way. For some, the grief is intensely private and not easily shared. Others find temporary respite from their grief in the company of friends and relations. Regardless of how we come to embrace our sorrow, it is, in Emily Dickenson's words *Solemnest of Industries Enacted upon Earth.*

> *What is sorrow for?*
> *It is a storehouse set*
> *On rocks for wheat, barley,*
> *corn and tears.*
> *One steps to the door on a round stone.*
> *The storehouse feeds*
> *all the birds of sorrow.*
> *And I say to myself: Will you have*
> *Sorrow at last?*
> *Go on, be cheerful in autumn,*
> *Be stoic, yes, be tranquil, calm,*
> *Or, in the valley of sorrows spread your*
> *Wings.* [2]
> Robert Bly

In my own process of sweeping up the heart, I turned for guidance to several familiar sources of literature on grief and loss. One was Robert Raines' *A Time to Live*, which I have referred to several times already. Raines used the poem quoted above as a focus for his chapter entitled *Embracing Sorrow*, which I found of particular help.

He explained how our own sorrow links us to the condition of others who suffer from grief and loss. Beyond that, it can sensitize us to both local and global issues and causes, such as hunger and poverty and global warming. By embracing our own sorrow, we become more empathetic and willing to take on the sorrows of the world rather than stand apart from them.

As the imagery in the poem suggests, sorrow acts as a storehouse, a large communal ground where we bring our grief and tears and heartache to be housed and nourished alongside those of others. We begin the first step of healing as we come to the door of the storehouse, ready to confront our grief there. We are freed both by and from our grief as we spread our wings in the valley of sorrows and let our stories go.

Sorrow will always remain a part of our experience. However, Raines encourages us to embrace it and incorporate it into our lives to create a rich tapestry in which the threads of joy and sorrow are woven tightly together to create a pattern that is rich in texture and color.

In the spirit of Bly's poem, I was moved to take a concrete step toward alleviating the sorrow of the poor and hungry. I decided to volunteer one day a week at Crisis Control Ministries, interviewing clients to establish the basis of their emergency and to determine if they meet the criteria for assistance. Crisis Control operates a pharmacy and a grocery store, and has funds to help with rent, utilities, and medication for clients who need emergency assistance. Bill and I have donated to Crisis Control for years and have been aware of the significant role the organization plays in the life of the community, but I had never spent any time there.

I completed the orientation process by shadowing an experienced interviewer for nine hours over the course of a week, to learn about the intake and application process. The next Monday, I shadowed a lead interviewer or supervisor who signs off on the applications, as well as approves assistance and writes checks, and completed my final training with Cynthia Fearrington, who is the Director of Client Services. I have enjoyed getting re-acquainted with Cynthia, who is also the mother of Matt, one of John Stillerman's friends from grade school. We have reminisced a lot about the hours we spent out at the Little League Park on Phillips Bridge Road, watching the boys and catching up on the gossip since the last season.

I still continue my volunteer work at Crisis Control every Monday morning from nine to noon and find it to be a satisfying way to make a small contribution to helping at least a few of the staggering number of people in poverty and need.

The loss of my brother-in-law and contemporary, made me keenly aware of the fleeting nature of time. I stopped procrastinating and made a lunch date with two of my favorite people—my sister Betsy and my longtime friend Carol from Charlotte days. Betsy and I met in Winston-Salem a week later to treat ourselves to pedicures and visit over lunch. Carol and I met at Davidson the week after that and it was such a pretty, sunny winter day, we ate our Panini and soup outside, on the porch of a great Italian restaurant called Campania. The times spent with my sister and with my old friend rejuvenated my spirit, and provided respite from grief.

In January, our family began the process of sweeping up the heart, of confronting our loss, and of weaving the joy and the sorrow together into our lives. It is a process that each will complete in his/her own way and in his/her own time.

CHAPTER 6

Resolution:

Wander and Explore New Pathways

Not all those who wander are lost. J.R.R. Tolkien

Getting Sidetracked

By February, I had drafted about forty pages in my memoir of Nonnie and decided to share it with my cousin Beth, who had published a novel entitled *The Beacon,* several years ago, when she and her husband John were pursuing a life of sailing and she was writing about their adventures. I had not yet let anyone but Bill read the draft, and I was anxious to receive some unbiased feedback that he would have been reluctant to provide. Beth was kind enough to read it and send it back with several good suggestions for revision, along with a few added tidbits about our grandmother told from the perspective of one who lived under the same roof with Nonnie throughout most of her (Beth's) childhood.

Beth was affirming of what I had written and encouraged me to finish it, as did my sister Betsy, who had been dabbling in some writing of her own, and to whom I had also sent a copy of the draft. I made up my mind to complete the memoir as originally intended, and then to build on that body of work and try my hand at developing a fictional character loosely based on Nonnie's life.

I had put my feelers out for a creative writing class to join—maybe at Wake Forest or Salem or Forsyth Tech—but had not been able to find exactly what I was looking for. In the meantime, I began searching the web for opportunities to hone my writing skills through some kind of online instruction. I discovered that there are numerous free classes offered online from many of the most prestigious universities on a variety of subjects, including writing.

While exploring the catalog of titles, I found an Old Testament survey course offered by Yale Divinity School and became completely distracted from my writing project.[1] The professor is a woman named Christine Hayes, and she has developed twenty-four lectures on *the Old* Testament that are available in transcript, audio, and video. I began reading the lectures and then watching them, and I could not pry myself away.

I spent almost two weeks working my way through the material, stopping just long enough to make the bed, clean the dishes, and get dinner on before Bill came home at night. Immediately after finishing the twenty-four lessons, I started on the companion course entitled *New Testament History and Literature*, taught by Dale Martin, also of Yale Divinity School. His course was equally compelling. My son Robert, a third year student at Wake Divinity School, lent me his study Bible to assist in following along with the readings. It had been ages since I had done any systematic study of The Bible—probably as far back as the Old and New Testament courses I took at Furman. I think once I did try to work my way through L.D. Johnson's book on covering The Bible in a year, but never made it too far past **Genesis.**

The Biblical instruction I have received over the years in Sunday school and church has been random and unconnected. The result is that there is a whole play list of scriptures stored up there in the *I-tunes* section of my brain and it is as if somebody put them on shuffle before they pressed the play button. I know about the shuffle button now. That is actually how I listened to the audio tape of *Harry Potter and the Sorcerer's Stone* some years back. I commented to my son Todd that the book made no sense at all the way it kept jumping around. Todd just shook his head and said, "Mom, you probably have it on shuffle." Indeed, I did, and what a difference it made when I located the shuffle button and turned it off. That is how I felt listening to the lectures. It was like somebody took the scriptures off shuffle for me.

The month of February was almost spent before my thoughts began to drift back to the Nonnie Project. I had accomplished little more than to re-read the draft that had sat idle for almost a month, when once again my road diverged, and I took the path that would lead to the discovery of my family roots.

Poerschke Family Tree

I was sorting through one of the boxes of photos and records that I had brought home from the storage unit, when I discovered a twelve-page, single-typed document on the Poerschke family, written as a letter and dated September 24, 1957. As I perused the document, with the assistance of the *Google* translator, it became clear that the author was Uncle Fritz Poerschke, my granddaddy's youngest brother. The letter is addressed to his *Liebe Kinder* (dear children), his sons Verner and Fred and daughter Esther-Ruth. He tells them that he is writing this *Pedigree* of the Poerschkes so *that when their parents no longer dwell on this earth, they will know where their parents and grandparents came from*. He explains that his early sources of the family came from information gathered by Helmut Schilling, the son of his sister Minna, who in 1943 took a bicycle trip to East Prussia to find out about his ancestors.

I had only been with Uncle Fritz a couple of times—once when I was a very young child, on one of our trips to Texas to see all of my dad's relatives, and then again, when he, Aunt Esther, and their daughter Esther-Ruth visited us in Siler City, North Carolina, in about 1958.

I remember him as a shorter and more stoutly built version of my grandfather. He was completely bald, whereas my grandfather retained his beautiful silver head of hair that was slightly receding in the front, forming a kind of widow's peak. Uncle Fritz tended to be brusque and businesslike, where my grandfather was warm and social. However, both brothers gazed through those familiar penetrating blue eyes that peered out from under the deeply furrowed brow, signature traits of the Poerschke family. My dad inherited the look, the brow, and blue eyes, traits that have continued to be dominant in the gene pool of his progeny, each of whom has inherited one or all of them.

Uncle Fritz spoke with a thick accent and still conversed in German as often as he did in English. His son Werner once laughingly commented that his dad had made little effort to perfect his English and that, even though he had been in the United States for over fifty years, he sounded like he *just got off the boat*. Based on that, it makes sense that his account of the Poerschke family origins would have been penned in the mother tongue.

Although my dad spoke fluent German and I heard my grandparents converse in it when they were arguing and did not want my sister and me to know what they were saying, my understanding of the language was limited to a few nursery rhymes and jingles that my grandmother taught us. As I struggled to make sense of the twelve-page letter, I deeply regretted that I had not taken the time to absorb the language as a child when there were so many native speakers around, or at least to have chosen German over French as my foreign language of choice in college. Alas, as I had not, it took me two full days with a German dictionary and the *Google Translate* program to piece together a rudimentary English translation. However, in the process, I learned a great deal about the origin of the Poerschke family and became aware of a vulnerable and reflective side of My Uncle Fritz, revealed in his commentary and side comments that accompanied his historical text.

I learned that the first Poerschkes can be traced back to East Prussia, which is now Poland. They lived very near the Russian border, not far from the Baltic Sea. Our Poerschkes had moved to Berlin by at least 1887, when Great-grandfather Gottfried and great-grandmother Louise were married. We know they were married in Berlin and that my grandfather Ernst was born there in 1888.

Berlin is about four hundred and thirty miles from where they lived in East Prussia. Gottfried Poerschke was born in 1860, in a town called Sillignnen and Louise Reckliehs was born in 1860, in Rastenburgh. The names of all locations in that area were changed by Hitler in the thirties and may have been changed again when East Prussia became a part of modern day Poland.

For most of the years that Gottfried and Louise lived in East Prussia, it was joined with West Prussia and the conjoined areas were known as The Province of Prussia (1829-1878). We have no record of how the first Poerschkes came to settle in East Prussia. It is likely that they may have come in during a wave of immigration following the famine and plague of 1709-11. One-third of the population died during this plague and, as a result, Crown Prince Frederick William I led the rebuilding and began to establish new towns. [2]

Thousands of Protestants expelled from the Archbishopric of Salzburg were allowed to settle in the depleted area. Our Poerschkes may well have come in on that wave. The original inhabitants, the Balts, were conquered by the Teutonic Knights. Many of them became Christianized. Over the centuries, Germanization and colonization resulted in the dominant group becoming German, with Poles and Lithuanians in the minority.[3]

We know that our Poerschkes in East Prussia dated back before 1797, when Christoph Poerschke was born to Christian Poerschke and Dorothea Shronter in the town of Sillginnen.

The Poerschke family became a part of a movement called the *Ostflucht*, or flight from the East, which began in 1850. Between 1850 and 1907, about 2.3 million East Prussians moved to find work in the industrial centers in the Ruhr and Berlin. The population in Berlin, where our Poerschkes settled, increased by 1.2 million during that time.

Our Poerschkes moved to Berlin after Gottfried's father, Gottfried I, contracted cholera and died December 6, 1886, leaving behind his wife Justine and four children. Industrialization had come to Germany and wages in the cities were good. Justine and the children, along with their spouses, moved from East Prussia and the farm to Berlin. Justine pined for her husband and the old land, and died on December 4, 1891 only five years after Gottfried's death.

The children adapted quickly to life in the city. Gottfried II was twenty-seven, when he married Louise Reckliehs in Berlin. Their home was on Timber Market Street in East Berlin. It was in that house that my grandfather Ernst was born. They went to the Baptist Church and were married and baptized by Julius Koebner. They were probably Particular Baptists and the church was probably one of the first Baptist churches in Germany.

I had known of the circumstances of my grandfather's immigration to America in 1910 since I was a child. He told me very frankly that he came in pursuit of my grandmother, whom he had met at church, and who had arranged to take a position as cook and nanny with a family in Texas. When he asked her to marry him, she said she would be glad to, but only if he would come to America first. He finished his education and apprenticeship in Berlin, and then set sail as a passenger on the *Hanover* from the port of Bremen, for Galveston, Texas, where he arrived on June 24, 1910.

What I did not know was that Fritz remained in Germany and was conscripted into the German army at twenty, in 1915. He was taken as a prisoner of war in 1917, after the Battle of Cambrai, the first battle in which the English used tanks. When he was released after the war, he and his fiancé Lizzie were married in 1920 and their son Werner was born in 1922. Fritz was a carpenter and made all of the furnishings in their apartment in Berlin. He wrote that the economy became so inflated after the war, especially in a country on the losing side, that money was worth nothing and employment was hard to find.

They reluctantly decided to leave their home and move to America, after Ernst sent them tickets for passage. Fritz wrote that they gave away most of their belongings and sold the beautiful kitchen set that he had made, for the price of a pocket watch and material for a dress for Lizzie.

They lived with my grandparents in Port Arthur until they could find work and then located in Beaumont and later in Houston, where Fritz worked until his retirement. A second son, Fred Willie, was born in 1932. Lizzie died of stomach cancer in 1943, when Fred was only twelve years old. For a time, he went to live with my grandparents in Port Arthur and became very close with them and with my father. When Uncle Fritz married Ester Burnhausen in 1945, he returned to live with his father. Ester and Fritz had a child together in June of 1945, the same year I was born.

Fritz also wrote of how my grandfather's sister Mieze and her husband Eric Faerber came from Berlin to

America in 1926, with their daughter Irmgard (Irma) who was born in 1918, the same year as my father. They lived briefly with my grandparents until Uncle Eric found work as an engineer with Humble Oil in Baytown, Texas. With the onset of the Depression, he was transferred to another plant and became unhappy with his employment situation.

In 1934, the year before Adolf Hitler rose to power, the World Baptist Congress was held in Berlin. The Faerbers booked passage to attend the conference. Once back in Berlin, they discovered that Germany was experiencing an economic boom. Uncle Eric found work and decided to stay in Germany, in Bad Oeyenhausen, where he and Meize lived out the remainder of their lives.

Irma, their only child, began her career as a correspondent in a news office in Berlin. She recounted to Bill and me once when she was retired and visiting in our home, that in the early years of Hitler's rise, everyone in Berlin had started to greet one another with *Hiel, Hitler.* Irma and some of the younger associates made light of it openly and refused to join in, until her boss took her aside and told her that she may be jeopardizing her safety by showing that kind of resistance. Irma considered that she was only engaging in her right to free speech and was shocked that her actions might be interpreted as resistance. It was a sobering hint of what was to come.

Irma soon found that she would have to get out of the reporting business.

After World War II, she moved back to the US and took a job with Avon Cosmetics. She rose quickly in the company and acquired a position as the head of their German advertising division. Her office was in York City but she spent a good portion of her time in Germany. This offered her the best of both worlds, as it enabled her to see her parents frequently and keep up with her German contacts.

Irma never married. She lived in Mamaronek, New York, and eventually retired from Avon and moved to Leyden, Massachusetts, with her German housekeeper Kayta and her beloved cats. We did not see Irma very often, but the few times she visited our family, she was great company and a delight to be around.

I met Uncle Eric and Aunt Meize only once, in 1960, when they visited in our home in Jacksonville, Florida. It was very shortly after my grandfather had died from pancreatic cancer and we were all still reeling from his death. I do not recall that I had ever been shown a picture of Aunt Meize, but when she got off the plane with Uncle Eric, I was unprepared for what I saw. I thought that my grandfather Ernst had been reincarnated in the body of a woman.

She was so much like him it was uncanny. Her walk, her bearing, her mannerisms, and her physical features, right down to the piercing blue Poerschke eyes and furrowed brow, were a feminine version of his. My sister and I were mesmerized by her and could not stop watching her and drinking her in. It was like having our grandfather back for a few sweet hours.

Family Roots

Other things may change us, but we start and end with the family. Anthony Brandt

After translating Uncle Fritz's Poerschke history, I became inspired to do some research on my own and I began looking into web sites that would allow me to trace the ancestry of the other branches of Bill's and my family tree. When I found *Ancestry.com*, I became submerged in their data and did not resurface until the end of March.

I have never been so addicted to a project. I would rise early to get a head start, and in what seemed like only a few minutes, I would look up and it would be lunchtime. I would tear myself away from the computer and complete a few chores, or run several errands, start supper, and then go right back to work. In a flash, it would be dark, and I would hear Bill's car coming up the driveway at the end of the day. After dinner, I would steal away to the computer for a few more hours, and there were even some nights after I had gone to bed, that I would wake up and go back to it again. One of the volunteers who I work with at Crisis Control Ministries had discovered *Ancestry.com* before I did. I commented to her one morning about how enthralled I had become with it. Her eyes brightened and she nodded her head vigorously in response. "I know," she admitted, blushing. "When I start working on that thing, time just evaporates."

Ancestry.com advertises itself as an online family resource that offers access to billions of digitized historical records, stories, and family trees. For a monthly membership fee, the user can access data that includes ship passenger lists, Social Security Death Records, military draft lists, US Census Records through 1940, immigration lists, etc. Members can also access the web sites of other members who have chosen to make their family trees public.[4]

The site allows the user to organize personal information in a family tree format and upload documents, pictures, and stories, and attach them to the individual family members on the tree. As each family member is entered, a green leaf appears beside the name whenever there is a record stored in the *Ancestry.com* data bank that relates to the person. The green leaf is called a *hint*, which will lead directly to that record by clicking the icon. Many of the documents, such as passenger lists and census records, can be viewed in their original handwritten form by clicking *view original document*, and it is possible to scroll up and down the pages for additional information.

I began with my dad's side of the family and entered what I knew about the Poerschkes, with help from Uncle Fritz's history and a notebook of documents from my dad's things. It was fairly easy to trace and record the Poerschke family tree back to 1797, and the birth of Christoph Poerschke in East Prussia. I was only able to trace the Kemnitz roots back to 1844, when my grandmother's father Karl Kemnitz was born in Lichtenburg, Germany, which is northeast of Munich. Her mother, Anna Klein-Gunther was born in 1853 somewhere in Germany, birthplace unknown.

I found the passenger list from the ship that my grandmother and her brother Heinrich sailed over on in 1908, as well as the census record listing her as cook in the home of an O'Connor family in Dallas in 1910. I also located the list from my grandfather's passage in 1910. With the click of a mouse, I was able to attach all of these records to the appropriate family member profiles, thus preserving it for posterity.

Next, I started to work on my mother's branch of the family. I had some help with names and dates on the Bryant side, my grandmother's, as Nonnie had written and published a memoir of her mother and father entitled *My Dearest One*, back in 1955.[5]

The Kendrick tree, my grandfather's side, had been traced by other members of the family and there was quite a lot of information on the member web sites that I was able to pick up and use. Some of the Kendrick research traces back to Captain John Kendrick, who discovered the Colorado River in 1773, but I have not established any connection to him from our branch of the family.

Judging from the number of green leaf hints, it appears that in the 1950's and 1960's, a primary motivation for tracing the family roots was to qualify for membership in the Daughters of the American Revolution, and in the case of the southern relatives, in the Daughters of the Confederacy.

Most of the eligible men on my mother's side of the family fought in the Revolution on the side of the Patriots and in the Civil War on the side of the Confederacy. My grandfather's father, Isham Kendrick (1835-1892), fought during the Civil War with D Company in the Sixteenth

South Carolina Regiment. In poor health after the Battle of Atlanta, he was put in charge of the effort to capture the *outliers,* deserters, and men without leave, in the upper section of Greenville County.

Isham's father, Isham (1755-1818), was reported to have enlisted and served as a private with the North Carolina troops, under Captain Sterling Clark and Major Charles Davis, and was in the Battle of Cowpens and Hillsboro.

My grandfather's grandmother was Suzannah Few (1803-1884); and her grandfather, James Few (1746-1771) was captain of a band of Regulators, fighting against Governor Tryon's troops at Alamance, over taxation and local control. Captured and hanged in 1771, about five miles from the battle, he was identified by historian George Bancroft as the first martyr to the cause of Independence.

My grandfather's mother was Julia Gilreath (1836-1884), whose great-grandfather, William Gilreath (1730-1795), served as a captain in the Revolutionary War and was wounded in the leg during the Battle of Kings Mountain.

My grandmother recorded in her book *My Dearest One* that her grandfather, Talbert Bryant (1839-1900), fought in the Battle of Gettysburg where part of his right hand was shot off. *He was taken prisoner there and was in prison for six months. He lived in such filth that he became infested with vermin. When he was released, he had no way to get home but to walk from Gettysburg to Anderson County. He had to beg for food and had only the clothes on his back. One night, he was holding his shirt over the fire to burn out the lice, and the shirt ignited and burned. He had to beg clothing to wear the rest of the way home. When he finally reached home, his feet were bleeding, his clothes were in rags, and his beard was long and unkempt. His wife Elizabeth said he hardly looked like a human being.*[5]

My grandmother's maternal grandfather was George Franklin Robinson (1834-1885) who served in the Civil War as a private with the 7th South Carolina Infantry Regiment Company A. Her maternal grandmother was Elvira Jane Griffin (1840-1921), whose Grandfather James Trotter (1725-1782) was a Sargeant in the Virginia militia during the Revolution. Her other maternal grandfather, Richard J. Fields (1758-1842) was a Private in the Light Horse (cavalry) in Randolph County, North Carolina, during the Revolution.

Both branches of my mother's family had immigrated to the United States during the late sixteen and early seventeen hundreds from England and Scotland

and Germany. From various locations in Virginia and Pennsylvania, they migrated down into North Carolina, and finally into South Carolina, where by the mid-eighteen hundreds, they had settled permanently in Pickens and Anderson Counties, and around Greenville. They were primarily small farmers, entrepreneurs, business people, and professionals whose lives revolved around their families, their churches, and their communities.

As I began researching Bill's family, I found that his story paralleled mine in a number of ways, only in different regions of the country. Both of our fathers were second-generation immigrants, whose parents had come to the U.S. in the early 1900's. My father's parents, who were German and Baptist, had sailed from Bremen to Galveston in 1908 and 1910, and settled in Port Arthur. Bill's father Hy's parents, who were Russian and Jewish, had sailed from Georgia to New York, in 1905, where they settled in Brooklyn. I have many more details about my dad's family, thanks to Uncle Fritz's history of the Poerschkes.

Thus far, my findings on Hy's family roots have been scant and I have only been able to trace them back using the *Ancestry.com* data to his father, David Stillerman (1870-) and his mother Rose Stillerman (1879-) and their arrival in New York in 1905. One additional piece of information comes from the 1930 census, which lists David as living in Brooklyn, head of the household, fifty-seven years old, and a carpenter by trade. Rose is listed as his wife and her age is recorded as thirty-three years. I am optimistic that other Stillerman relatives possess personal records and documents on David and Rose, and that once I have access to them, I will be able to fill in some of the blanks.

Both of our mothers' families had been among the early colonists and had migrated from Virginia, south and west to new settlements. They had fought in the Revolutionary War as Patriots and in the Civil War, albeit on different sides. Whereas my mother's family ended up in South Carolina in Anderson and Pickens County, Bill's mother Margie's family took a westward turn after they migrated to North Carolina, and headed for Tennessee, Kentucky, and finally Illinois.

Both of our mothers' families were Protestant, mostly Baptists and Methodists. One of Bill's ancestors, Constant Powell, used his team of oxen to haul the bricks to build the first Methodist Church in Illinois, in the settlement at Shiloh. Most of the Powells were buried in the cemetery across from that church, with the exception of Constant's great grandson, William Constant, who had moved with his family to Phoenix, Arizona, and was buried there. One of my ancestors, BF Few, helped to organize the first Methodist Church in Greer, South Carolina. His Son, William Preston Few became the first president of Duke University.

My grandmother had written her Bryant and Robinson family history in 1955. Likewise, back in the fifties, Bill's grandmother Cora and her sister Blanche had researched their Powell and Dale relatives and had written up their findings for the family members. This information was extremely helpful when paired with the *Ancestry.com* data bank.

The Powell name is quite prominent in the history of the American colonies and included wealthy ship owners and commanders. Our Powells probably descended from Captain Thomas Powell (1599-1687), who was born in Suffolk, England, and died on the Isle of Wight, Virginia. If the line is correct, it continues back to Powells in Jamestown who came from England and earlier Wales. At any rate, we can confirm that the early Powells, Hampton Powell (1773-1852), who was born in Halifax County, North Carolina, and wife Sally (1785-1850), who was born in Edgecombe County, moved from North Carolina to Montgomery, Tennessee, where their son Constant Powell (1806-1866) was born and raised.

When Constant was about thirty-two, he attended a campground revival held by a Baptist circuit rider. He was converted and, as a part of his new belief, became an abolitionist. He sold his slaves and moved his family by covered wagon, pulled by oxen, to the settlement of New Design, Illinois. He moved there to join a Baptist church organized in 1789, by a Reverend James Leman, who was also an abolitionist. Constant later moved to O'Fallon, Illinois, to work on the railroad there. Constant's son William Henry (1844-1883) enlisted in the 17th Illinois Volunteer Infantry company I, and fought in the Civil War on the side of the Union. His company engaged in campaigns in Tennessee, Arkansas, and Louisiana.

The Dale family also were among the early colonists. William Dale (1757-1822) was a veteran of the Revolutionary War, where he had served under Captain Henry Fauntleroy's regiment, and was present at the surrender of Lord Cornwallis at Yorktown. After the war, he and his wife Elizabeth set off across the mountains to join Daniel Boone's movement to settle Kentucky. William died in 1822, and his son Lewis moved the family to Illinois and settled new land there. Lewis and his wife had a daughter, Mary Ellen Dale (1844-). In 1860, both parents died of cholera, and Mary Ellen was sent to live first with a sister, on the prairie, and then with a family by the name of Christy, who lived in St. Louis. The Christy's moved to O'Fallon and Mary Ellen went with them. It was there that she met and married William Henry Powell, who had just returned from the Civil War. William Henry Powell and Mary Ellen Dale were Bill's grandmother Cora's grandparents.

William died of consumption in 1883. Mary Ellen stayed on in O'Fallon for a while; but she eventually moved to Collinsville, Illinois to be closer to her daughter Ora and her son William Constant, who had already moved there. William Constant Powell was Cora's father and Margie's grandfather.

There was not a great deal to be found on Margie's father, William Mathias (1888-1976), except that he was the second of four children of James Mathias (1863-1932) and Anna Talbert (1869-1918). Both parents were born near Springfield, north of St. Louis, and they lived their lives in and around the town of Collinsville, Illinois.

There is, however, a very interesting story about James Mathias, who apparently became an unwilling participant in the Great Collinsville Mail Robbery of 1925. I acquired the story from a newspaper clipping passed on to me by Bill's mother Margie that was written by KL Monroe, in a column entitled *As I See It*, in the Collinsville paper, no date attached. The facts and circumstances contain all of the elements for good fiction, and would make a great movie or short story.

The Great Collinsville Mail Robbery

It was during the prohibition era, when bootlegging and racketeering and gang wars ran rampant. The Shelton Brothers—Carl, Earl, and Bernie—and the Charlie Birger gang with Art Newman, joined forces to carry out their illegal operations. They later split over the division of their take from the Williamson County slot machines.[6]

Much of the activity centered in Williamson County, southeast of St. Louis, where, despite a bloody history of feuds and mine union violence, there had not been a conviction for murder for a hundred years. Things had gotten so bad there that an ex-prohibition agent *reformer* S. Glenn Young was able to rally a mob of thousands of Klansmen, inspired by the White Anglo-Saxon Protestant ministers of the county, to take control and go after the gangs.

In response, the Shelton brothers and the Birger gang joined some of the regular law enforcement establishment to take on Young and the Klan, resulting in the murder of at least twenty-nine men and women. The bootlegging and racketeering played out between 1923 and 1928; however, the Great Mail Robbery in Collinsville was the only event in the gang wars that resulted in the Shelton boys being sentenced or serving time.

On the morning of January 27, 1925, James Mathias picked up the pouches at the Pennsylvania depot at the foot of Reed Avenue and headed toward the Post Office. He turned off of Church Street onto Chestnut Street. A big Buick with side curtains was waiting on Church. It pulled alongside Mathias and forced him to the curb a half a block from Main Street. Two bandits jumped on the running board and ordered Mathias to put his hands up and his head down. They rooted among the pouches for the one they wanted, grabbed it and one other, went back to their waiting car, sped down Main Street, and headed off to East St. Louis via Caseyville Road.

The bag contained fifteen-thousand dollars ordered from the National Bank of Commerce in St. Louis through the Federal Reserve to cover the Lumaghi Mine payroll. The bank had thirty-thousand dollars on deposit there, and needed the other fifteen-thousand dollars to cover.

By this time, the Sheltons and the Birgers were mortal enemies. Birger attempted to pin the Collinsville robbery on Shelton by convincing a postal inspector that they were guilty.

Despite the fact that James Mathias, James Purcell, assistant cashier of the State Bank who was thirty feet from the ford truck when it was robbed, and baker Adolph

Meyer who saw the car, all said that they could not recognize the Shelton brothers, the Sheltons were convicted on the testimony of Charlie Birger and Art Newman. They claimed that Shelton had invited them to take part in the robbery and that he later saw them splitting some of the money at Shady Rest, Birger's hideout where they were running their bootlegging

A key witness was Harvey Dungey, who claimed to be an East St. Louis cab driver but was really Birger's liquor runner. He tied the Sheltons to Collinsville by saying that he had seen them with the hood up trying to fix the Buick used in the robbery.

The three Sheltons were sentenced to federal prison at Leavenworth where they stayed only thirty days when St. Louis Post-Dispatch writer John T. Rogers found out that Dungey was really in Oklahoma City on the day of the robbery.

I have included only a few examples from the *Ancestry.com* search that lured me off the main road that I had been traveling and led me to the Poerschke-Stillerman family roots. By the end of March, I had completed a preliminary investigation on both branches of the family, had attached pictures and documents to each individual family member's profile, and had written a short narrative summarizing my findings. I e-mailed copies to my children, my sister, and my cousin Beth, and sent a hard copy of the narrative to Bill's mother Margie. I was not ready to go public with the website, but I e-mailed the link and password to my website to all of them so that they could access it, edit, and add information. There is a great deal more to be discovered about the Poerschkes and the Stillermans; but now, we at least have a digitized account of our family, which can be built upon in years to come.

A Language Dilemma

I have always been fascinated with languages, and have dabbled in a few other than English, but have never become proficient. That has not stopped me from fantasizing that someday I would. All of this exposure to my Poerschke roots had me scheming about how I could learn sufficient German to communicate well enough to navigate the streets of Berlin and find the place on Timber Market Street where my grandfather Ernst was born. I was pretty sure I could talk my son Robert, my father's namesake, into going with me, especially if we took in Oktoberfest. It would be the perfect way to combine my love of language with my love of travel and interest in family history.

And then, there is that dream I have had since my trip to Italy, when I completely fell in love with the Italian Language, which I had learned just enough of to ask how to get to the bathroom and to order a cappuccino. I fantasized for months about how I would work through all of the Pimsleur Language tapes and absorb enough Italian to go to language school in Siena, perhaps one with a culinary emphasis including lessons on Italian cooking.

However, it is the French language in which I have had the most formal training, and in which I actually taught a conversational class my first year of teaching, God bless my poor students! I took three years of French at Shades Valley High School, in Birmingham, with Miss Tidwell, who was always waving her arms and shouting in Alabama French *C'est terrible!* (that's terrible) and *Taisez-vous !* (shut up!). At Furman, I came within three credit hours of a major in French, but decided at the last minute on history instead. After all that, when I finally took my dream trip to Paris almost forty years later, I could not even remember how to say, *Check, please.* That did not stop me from reading and pronouncing aloud every French sign, like a toddler practicing her words, and from perking up every time I was able to recognize even one or two phrases from the conversations of the native speakers passing by. I loved the sights and the sounds of Paris.

Finally, there is Spanish. It is not a language I have fantasized about learning in conjunction with tripping all over the globe and taking in all the sights and sounds of foreign places. The Spanish language is one that has confronted me daily right here at home. My failure to learn it had already begun to impede my ability as a principal to communicate with the growing number of Hispanic students and their families enrolled in my school. It continues to be a barrier in my volunteer work at Crisis Control Ministries, with the significant number of Hispanic clients who require English translation. Spanish is the language that my conscience tells me I must learn if I am serious about reaching out to and identifying with those of my fellow human beings who are members of the fastest growing cultural minority group in America, and who along with other minority groups receive a disproportionate slice of the economic pie.

Throughout my career as an educator, a primary goal was to maintain a level educational playing field in the school by removing or at least minimizing the barriers of cultural bias and economic disadvantagement, two of the major obstacles to my students' learning. In recent years, I discerned a third obstacle, that of language, with my second language students, who were predominantly Hispanic. Over half of those students were undocumented immigrants for whom the US immigration laws would ultimately become a fourth barrier.

East Middle had one of the largest enrollments of Hispanic students in the Iredell Statesville School system, a number that had increased dramatically during my twelve-year tenure there, reflecting the significant growth trend in the Hispanic population across the state. According to the 2010 US Census, the Hispanic population in North Carolina grew from around 8 million to around 9.5 million, an increase of 111.1%.[7] Though we received a large number of students from Colombia in past years, the majority in more recent years were Mexican in origin, also reflecting the national statistics of Mexicans accounting for 65% of Hispanic growth in population since the 2000 census.

A large percentage of our students had been born in the United States or had moved here at an early age. Most had become proficient with English and, and as one of the subgroups measured by the *No Child Left Behind* standards, which have now been mercifully amended, they always showed positive yearly gains. Our Hispanic students learned quickly and did quite well socially and academically in school where they communicated in English. Whereas they were bilingual, many of their parents had not even begun to master English. When they went home, it was often to an environment where Spanish was spoken exclusively.

Language became a huge barrier to creating a strong partnership between school and home, which is such an essential component of student success. Unfortunately, most of the school personnel, me included, were, like our students' parents, not bilingual. Thus, we had to rely on the itinerant Spanish translator hired by the system, on the days she was assigned to us, or pull our overworked ESL teacher Edmundo Rosas from instruction, on days when she was not available, to assist in translation during parent/teacher/administrator conferences. Of course, we had a ready supply of bilingual students available, but for reasons of confidentiality, we could not always involve them.

On one occasion, a sixth grade boy was sent to my office after multiple incidents of sassing his teacher and disrupting the class. I was at my desk and he was sitting in the *hot seat* across from me, his chubby brown arms folded, his tennis shoes swinging back and forth about two inches from the floor. The dark eyes peered out from under tousled bangs and he rolled them nonchalantly to hide his terror at being called to the principal's office

I lectured him sternly on his behavior and followed up by asking, "Is your mother at home?"

He nodded affirmatively.

I finished my remonstration with the words I had delivered to a hundred other little sixth grade boys who had sat in that same seat for the same reason.

"Good. Well, then, I'm just going to call her and see how she feels about her son disrespecting his teacher and keeping the other students from learning because you insist on being the class clown. I know she taught you better than that, and we'll just see what she has to say."

"No, you can't do that," he replied. "She does not speak English."

The Spanish translator was not around that day, and I did not feel the circumstances warranted pulling Mr. Rosas away from his students to call this child's mother for the sole purpose of giving him a good scare. I was foiled, but I decided to bluff my way through.

"Okay, then. I'm assuming that you speak Spanish." He nodded affirmatively again.

"In that case, I want you to come over here and pick up this phone and dial your mother yourself. You are going to tell her every single thing you have done and you had better not leave out one detail. And then, you are going to tell her she needs to make an appointment with your teacher for a conference, and I want to know the time and date she can come so I can arrange for Mr. Rosas to be there and translate." And finally I warned, "I can't speak Spanish, but I do know a few words, and I'll be able to tell if you aren't being honest with her."

That tactic worked pretty well as a measure for scaring small children temporarily into sitting still and listening to the teacher, until time and maturity could take over and enable them to do it independently. However, there were many instances where a subtler, more delicate approach was required, and in those instances, there was simply no substitute for being able to speak directly to, and in the same language of, the parent.

Language was not the only barrier confronting my students. Far worse were the barricades on the road to employment and higher education thrown up by United States Immigration Laws that would hit them down the road resulting from the undocumented status of their parents. Though they had lived in the United States for most or all of their lives and had attended American schools where, at least in North Carolina, they received the same access to a free public education as their cohorts who were natural born citizen, they would not be extended that opportunity indefinitely

As undocumented aliens, they could not apply for a legal driver's license when they turned sixteen, or on high school graduation, claim in-state tuition at a community college or university without risking deportation. Even the documented students could not qualify for federal aid if they had not received a green card. If they wanted to further themselves, they were placed in the precarious position of driving their cars illegally to jobs that paid minimum wage in order to earn enough money to pay out of state tuition.

The United States Immigration system is in desperate need of reform, and I am no expert on how to do that. I certainly support the view that we must keep drug dealers and terrorists out of our country; and, I do not have a problem with a strict deportation policy for aliens who break the law. I even sympathize with the view that we should not bend the rules for those who achieve entry by illegal means when there are those who have followed legal procedure and waited patiently to become citizens. But, surely, we can find a way to pass responsible immigration laws that assist rather than penalize this large group of youths in their effort to obtain the skills and knowledge that will enable them to make their mark on their community and world.

I have experienced firsthand how language and the United States Immigration laws can stand in the way of opportunity for the fastest growing segment of our population. Now that I have retired, I will continue to look for ways to remove these barriers to Hispanic Americans as a group, by advocating for reforms to immigration like those included in the recently defeated DREAM Act, and individually, as I work with Hispanic families through Crisis Control Ministries to provide assistance in their time of need. All that being said, I needed to stop fantasizing and get busy learning Spanish.

I took the first step in that direction by researching available Spanish language learning programs. I had some experience with the *Pimsleur Program* in Italian and Spanish, and had worked with *the Rosetta Stone* in French as well. However, the one I settled on was *Speed Learning Languages*, which is a set of courses available in French, Spanish, German, Italian, and Chinese (Mandarin), developed by the US government for diplomats and government officials seeking to gain rapid proficiency in speaking a foreign language. The program was highly rated by a number of internet sources and was much more reasonably priced than *Pimsleur* or *Rosetta Stone*.[8]

I purchased and downloaded the program onto my desktop and started working through the first few lessons.

At that time, I was finishing the online courses in Old and New Testament mentioned previously, and was becoming immersed in the *Ancestry.com* project, which would for the next month consume my interest as well as the bulk of my time. I decided to put the Spanish lessons on hold for a while, until I could discipline myself to spend at least an hour every day working through the material. I felt certain that I could make rapid progress under those conditions, since I had previously studied French, one of the romance languages, and had learned a number of words and basic phrases in Spanish as well. The shortcut icon for the program remains on my desktop, as a reminder of my new resolution to learn some Spanish.

Patsy Ann

As I was pouring through family pictures and documents in conjunction with the *Ancestry.com* search, I found a large shoebox, stored among the rest of the memorabilia. Opening it, I realized that it contained the remains of a doll called Patsy Ann that had been my mother's favorite childhood toy. I do not know who gave my mother the doll or the circumstances surrounding the gift. However, I do know that it was the only doll my mother ever played with and that she had loved Patsy Ann dearly.

After my mother died in 1992, we were going through her drawers and her personal things. The doll was one of the items I saved and brought home, thinking that one day, in the not too distant future, I would have her restored. Periodically, I would come across the box and it would remind me of my intention. Before I knew it, twenty years had passed and Patsy Ann was still lying there broken and unrepaired.

Patsy Ann had come apart and needed to be re-strung. One of her fingers and three of the toes on her left foot were broken, and her hair needed to be repainted. She looked pretty bad, lying there in pieces in the shoebox, and I came within an inch of tossing her out. But for some reason, I could not do it. After all, she had a name and a history, and even in her current state of dismemberment, there was something oddly appealing about her. She was not an infant, but looked like a child of about three years, with a plump roundness in her face and arms and legs. Her hair, which had been painted on, was styled in the popular bob of the day. It was worn in spots, and had faded from reddish to a dull brown. She had big green eyes and a small pouty mouth, like a tiny red rosebud. She was a fairly large doll, and when I laid her on the table and pieced her together, I judged that she had been about nineteen inches tall. On the back of the head was printed the word *Effanbee*, which was the name of the company that manufactured her.

I Googled *Effanbee* and *Patsy Ann Doll* and found an amazing web site called *PatsyAnn.Net*, fully devoted to the Patsy Ann doll just like my mother's. The collector's name is Debbie Wallace Essig, who claims that her love and fascination of dolls stems from the fact that they are more than childhood toys. *They give us a piece of history by putting a face to the culture in which they are created.*[9] Essig has posted color photos of restored dolls, dressed in the outfits of the 1930's and posed around period toy furniture. She refers to her site as an online museum. From the pictures, I was immediately able to visualize how much this toy must have delighted little girls, and I could understand why my mother had been attached to her Patsy Ann.

According to the website, the Patsy Ann Doll went on the market in 1929, just months prior to the Stock Market Crash in October. My mother was born in 1924, which would have made her five years old, if she got the doll the first year it came out. As I have written earlier, my grandfather, John Kendrick, suffered a complete breakdown as a result of losing his fortune in that crash.

He was in and out of the state mental hospital from that time until his death in 1935, and was never able to provide for his family again. The family lost their home, and my grandmother had to move to Greenville to seek employment to support her dependent children. It was an especially hard time for my mother's family as well as for the nation.

The creator of Patsy Ann was Bernard Lipfert, a doll sculptor, who was born in 1886, and emigrated from Germany to New York City, first to Brooklyn and later to Long Island. He worked as a freelance artist out of his basement and sold his work to various doll companies. He collaborated with the Effanbee Company, which produced the Patsy Ann Doll. The dolls were made of a material called composition, a mixture of wood pulp and glue, and were then painted. Composition dolls had a warm glow to them. The material was considered more durable than the bisque or wax, which had been used previously; however, it was found to chip and wear down over time; and, by the 1950's was replaced by hard plastic.

The first Patsy Ann Dolls sold for around five dollars, and often, as a Depression era marketing strategy, could be had for the purchase of a newspaper subscription or the opening of a bank account. The Effanbee Company began a new trend of manufacturing separate clothing and wardrobes for the dolls in the Patsy family, to promote sales throughout the year. Clothing patterns were developed by the major companies for home sewing as well. Patsy Ann had her own book, *Patsy Ann, Her Happy Times* by Mona Reed King, published in 1936 by Rand McNally.[10]

After reading about the background of the doll and seeing the pictures of the restored Patsy Ann dolls on the web page, I decided to look in to having my mother's Patsy Ann restored, and found a place called The Doll Hospital, at *dollsbydiane.com*, that looked promising. I watched the animated video of *Paul, the doll doctor* giving instructions on how to pack and ship a doll patient in need of repair. I carefully packed up my mother's Patsy Ann Doll according to Dr. Paul's directions, printed out the mailing label provided right there on the web site, and sent her by UPS to Diane's Doll Hospital in Homosassa, Florida. Several days later, I received a call from Diane herself, informing me that Patsy Ann had arrived and was in good hands.[11]

I asked her if Patsy Ann could be repaired, and she replied that it would take a lot of work, but that they could certainly do it. Next, I held my breath and asked the bottom line question, "How much will it cost?" She estimated that it would take about three-hundred dollars to re-string her, repair the broken fingers and toes, and to re-paint the hair. For four-hundred dollars, they would return Patsy Ann to me fully outfitted, with undergarments, dress, pinafore, shoes and socks. The final price would also include a history of the doll and an appraisal of her worth, in case I ever wanted to sell her. Four-hundred dollars seemed like an awfully big investment for a doll with an original worth of five dollars. But Diane reminded me, that it was not the dollar value that had motivated me to pack her up and send her to the doll hospital.

She was right. Patsy Ann had a name and a history. She had been important to a little girl who grew up at a time when the nation and her world seemed to be coming apart at the seams. Too quickly, the girl got older and moved on to other things. Patsy Ann was outgrown but not completely forgotten. After over eighty years of family moves, rummage sales, spring cleanings, re-organizings, and de-clutterings, she survived the garbage pile and continued to be carried along and stored with the rest of the family memorabilia.

The voice on the end of the line broke my reverie, "Would you like for me to put this on your credit card, so that we can get started right away? We can have her back to you in about four weeks."

As I struggled to justify the expense, I thought of Peter Walsh's rule about hanging on to possessions of dearly departed family members. Our memories of our loved ones do not reside in their possessions, but in our minds and hearts. If we intend on honoring an individual with an item that has been handed down to us, we must clean it up, make a proper place for it, and enjoy it. Otherwise, throw it out! Leaving it in a box to collect dust and mildew only causes clutter and frustration.

That settled it for me. I pulled out my wallet, found my Visa card and began reading off the numbers to Diane. She took down my billing information and we ended our conversation. As Diane had promised, four weeks later I received a package from the Doll Hospital in Homosassa, Florida. I tore into it right there on the front porch and found the new and improved Patsy Ann, arms and legs intact, freshly painted hair, and fully clad in starched white undergarments, printed cotton dress and pinafore, white socks, and black Mary Jane shoes. I scooped her up in my arms, carried her inside, and set her on the raised hearth in the kitchen. Patsy Ann was home and ready to be introduced to a new generation.

Even after her makeover, she shows definite signs of wear and tear, partially from love and partially from neglect. After all, she has been around for eighty-three years. But, she still stands upright, head tilted, plump little arms extended, with the same whimsical expression she always had. Like the irresistible three-year-old child she was created to resemble, she is waiting for a girl or boy to take her hand to go off to play. How can you put a price on that?

CHAPTER 7

Resolution: *Re-Define Work*

We work to become, not to acquire. Elbert Hubbard

One of my resolutions for the year was to reflect on my work history and to re-think and re-imagine the form and shape my work will take during the elder season. By May, I still had questions about where all of this would lead. Would my work be exclusively volunteer in nature or would I seek gainful employment? Would I find something to do related to my former career in education, or would I break new ground and do something entirely different? Would I learn a new skill? Go back to school? Start a business? Or, would I putter around and fill my days pursuing random interests and going from one project to the next?

The jury is still out on which pathway I will travel. However, I suspect that whatever work I do in the future will be grounded in the work that I have done in the past; and, thus, I begin with a reflection on my work life—how I have come to define it and how it has come to define me.

As one among the first crop of Baby Boomers, I grew up in a world where most little girls were destined to become wives, mothers, and homemakers. Women pursuing a career path generally had three options for employment: teacher, nurse, or secretary. There were, of course, women who studied for the professions of law and medicine, but they were in the minority and they received little encouragement.

My sister Betsy, who is four years my junior, showed an early interest in becoming a doctor. She kept a stuffed monkey for a patient that my grandmother had made from a pair of brown work socks with red heels and toes. He was already a pitiful looking thing, with an elongated head and long stringy arms and legs and tail. Grandmother must not have had quite enough cotton stuffing when she put him together, but she made do and finished him off anyway. He looked all the more pitiful hooked up to the makeshift IV that Betsy created out of a plastic bottle and some tubing. She laid him out on a green roller cart, which served as a gurney, and she rolled him all over the house, monitoring his pulse and other vital signs. Her interest in medicine continued beyond early childhood. She could name all of the bones in the body by the time she was eight years old.

My parents knew the odds she faced as a woman if she followed this career path, and they did everything they could to encourage her and praise her interest. Ironically, in their attempt to support what they thought was her dream, they communicated something entirely different. When Betsy decided not to pursue a pre-med course in college, she told them that she had only begun that course of study because she knew how much they wanted her to be a doctor and she did not want to disappoint them.

I, on the other hand, had no idea what I wanted to be when I grew up. I romanticized about finding a handsome husband and having lots of little *Gerber* babies with blond hair and blue eyes, and perfect little curls framing their faces. In terms of a career, I found the idea of being a secretary boring, and the notion of becoming a nurse was out of question, due to my aversion to blood. When I entered Furman, I chose, by default to prepare myself for teaching, but never dreamed that I would ever have to spend much time in the classroom.

I had not worked a day in my life, unless you count the two weeks over Christmas holidays, when I was twelve years old and earned fifty dollars wrapping packages and making change at Belk's Department Store in Siler City. I became pretty good at wrapping, but I was terrible at making change, and would probably have been fired if the manager had not been one of the deacons in our church and too nice to tell my Daddy that I was such a bad employee.

I did finally get a job on the switchboard at Furman my junior year, after much pressure from my parents to earn my own spending money; but, it began to interfere with my social life too much and I quit that after several months.

As a collegian, I was arrogant and overconfident, with very little reason to be that way. My friend Minnie's father had a saying that described me to the tee: *If I could buy you for what you are worth and sell you for what you think you're worth, I would make a fortune.* I cringe now as I remember announcing to poor, patient, Dr. King, my methods professor who had devoted his whole life to teaching, that I felt that teaching was intuitive and that it was a waste of time for us to have to sit through all these education courses. In actuality, I had heard an upper classman say that and liked the sound of it. I thought *intuitive* was a great word and I was trying it out on him.

Despite myself, I did manage to graduate from Furman with a BA in history and minors in French and secondary education. I moved back home with my parents and lucked up and got a job at Wake Forest High School for the coming year, at the last minute when Mrs. Barnes, the beloved US History teacher who had been at the school for years, suddenly developed a health problem that forced her into an early retirement. I was assigned to teach four sections of US History, one World History class, and a conversational French class.

Work was merely a sideline for me, as I was consumed with planning a December wedding and with spending every other available minute with Bill, who was enrolled at Southeastern Seminary and living in the single-students' dorm until our wedding.

There was nothing to do in Wake Forest, a tiny town just fifteen miles from Raleigh, and so we travelled almost every weekend to see our college friends. The seminary scheduled classes for Tuesday through Friday to accommodate the students who travelled to their churches on the weekends. Bill was not working in a church and he used Mondays for a study day. Many times, we would leave town on Friday afternoon and return late Sunday night in time for me to prepare for school the next day.

One Monday morning after being gone all weekend, I was taking the roll in my first period history class.

"Harvey Choplin," I called. No answer.

"Harvey Choplin", I repeated. Still no answer.

"Does anyone know where Harvey Choplin is?" I asked.

A voice from the back of the room replied flatly, "He's dead."

"Excuse me. What did you say?" I choked.

"He's dead. He got killed."

After recovering from my shock, I discovered from further inquiry that Harvey, a quiet student of modest means, had been in a terrible automobile accident on Friday night. He died instantly, was mourned on Saturday, and was buried on Sunday. This was one of my students. He was in his seat on Friday and was gone on Monday, and I had no clue about any of it.

I could fill a book with examples of my insensitivity and of the stupid things I did or did not do my first year of teaching, but that is not the purpose of this chapter. I include this incident about Harvey because I think it says it all about how disconnected I was to the whole business of teaching. My knowledge of subject matter, history, was decent; for I had studied at the feet of Delbert Gilpatrick, Winston Babb, Newton Jones, and Bill Leverette, all credible historians at Furman. I even *got by* in French with a pretty good accent and a textbook that was teacher proof. However, I totally lacked the skills of classroom management and method that Jacob Kounin, back in the seventies, summed up in the term *withitness*. Perhaps teaching was not as intuitive as I had thought.

I taught for another year at Wake Forest High School. Bill and I lived in a seminary duplex across the street from the school and I could literally hear the warning bell ring from our living room, as I scrambled out the door to get to my classes before the tardy bell sounded five minutes later. More often than not, I was late to school, a habit, which did not sit well with my principal.

When Bill accepted an internship with First Baptist Church in Smithfield, we moved to Johnston County, where I taught at North Johnston High School for my third and final year. In June of 1970, I gleefully left the teaching profession, cashed out my retirement, and spent all of the money on a week-long trip to New York City and New England for Bill and me. The next year I became pregnant with Todd, who was born August 31, 1971. For the following ten years, my work was primarily that of mother, homemaker, and wife.

We moved to Montgomery County in 1973, where Bill became pastor of the First Baptist Church of Mount Gilead. While we lived there, John was born in April of 1975 and Harry and Robert were born in June of 1977. Although Bill was a wonderful father and a hands-on dad, our marriage during those years was traditional, with a definite division of labor between the two of us. He was the breadwinner and provider and I was the stay-at-home mom and homemaker.

When Todd started kindergarten and before Harry and Robert were born, I dabbled a bit in teaching with a part time job at a private school in Wadesboro, and Bill helped out by picking John up from day care and Todd up from Kindergarten. But, for the most part, we kept to our roles, even though it was a strain on our resources to manage with only one breadwinner in the family. Additionally, the fact that we moved several times during those years for Bill to pursue his career, made it difficult for me to establish any kind of continuity or tenure as a teacher, even if I had been so inclined to seek work outside the home, which I clearly was not.

Toward the end of our stay in Mount Gilead, I became interested in the idea of pursuing a master's degree in history. As I had never entertained the slightest thought of doing graduate work when I was at Furman, I had declined the opportunity to take the Graduate Record Exam when my studies were fresh. Thus, I did not take it until ten years later as a pre-requisite to acceptance to the Master's program at UNC-Charlotte. My math score was terrible, but the verbal was high enough to compensate, and so I was accepted into the program.

I commuted about fifty miles from Mount Gilead to Charlotte, one night a week, to attend class from 6:00-9:00 pm. It was dark as pitch driving those country roads and Bill had a CB radio installed in my car in case I were ever to break down. Our church members thought it was scandalous that Bill was *letting me* drive all that way at night all by myself, but somebody had to stay at home with the kids and get them to bed, and he was the only one around to do it.

I finished twelve credit hours before we moved from Mount Gilead to Buie's Creek in 1978, and found the classes to be stimulating and enjoyable. One of my professors was Paul Escott, who went on to become the dean at Wake Forest, and another was Marianne Stroebel, who went on to chair the history department at Furman. They were fantastic teachers, exacting and demanding of their students. Both were experts on United States History and used literature to teach their content. I read my eyes off in their classes and had a chance to improve my writing skills as they critiqued my papers and offered feedback.

When we moved to Buie's Creek, I eventually completed my degree at Campbell University, whose campus was located a block from our house. Campbell did not offer a master's in history, but I was able to transfer most of my credits and use them toward a Masters in

Intermediate Education. That was vastly more practical, in that the opportunity for finding a teaching position in history that did not carry with it coaching responsibilities was slim to none.

The year I entered Campbell, the State of North Carolina passed a law, in response to Governor Hunt's reading initiative, to require all graduate programs in education to include at least one course in reading theory. As a former high school teacher, I grumbled loudly about the requirement. After all, I was a history teacher and I did not have time to teach my students what they should already have learned in elementary school. However, I found this course to be one of the most fascinating I had ever taken. For the first time, I learned that reading is far more than the mere sounding out and calling of words. It is an interactive process by which the reader makes meaning out of the text. We begin by learning to read, and progress to a level where we read to learn. Reading is comprehension. It is a thinking skill.

As an elective, I signed up for a course in Ornithology. It was offered in summer school, and we met every day for several weeks. We would start class, armed with binoculars and notebooks, by taking a walk and looking for birds indigenous to the area. We spotted red winged black birds, blue birds, grackles, songbirds, woodpeckers, and meadowlarks, among other species. We would then go into the classroom for lecture and, in the last hour, participate in a lab in which we learned to skin, preserve and mount a bird that had died from disease or been picked up on the road and stored in the biology department freezer to use as a lab specimen. It sounds disgusting, but I became so engrossed in taking apart my tiny little Yellow Throated Warbler, that I forgot to be squeamish.

We also took a field trip to the coast to see the Heron rookeries and the Pelicans nesting near Wilmington. To this day, I have retained my interest in birds sparked by that course. I keep my Roger Tory Peterson field guide nearby and look up any strange bird that enters the yard. Bill and I have hung several bird feeders in our back yard that we fill year round. We have done everything we could, to no avail, to outsmart the greedy squirrels, and have finally resigned ourselves to feeding them too.

In 1980, with all of the children enrolled at Buie's Creek Elementary School, I took a job in Fayetteville, at Pine Forest Junior High School, as a seventh grade language arts and social studies teacher. In 1967, I chose teaching by default. This time, I chose it because it was really what I wanted to do. I began to think of teaching as a career rather than just a job. I stayed at Pine Forest for five years, until we moved to Winston-Salem, where Bill became the President of Baptist Retirement Homes of North Carolina, Inc.

One of the highlights of my educational career was the opportunity to attend the North Carolina Writing Project at Pembroke University, in the summer of 1982. It was a three-week, eight-hour-a day institute for teachers that would revolutionize my teaching style and forever change the way I did business in the classroom. Participating in the institute also gave me a chance to hone my own writing skills in the context of a community of writers. The institute was based upon the Bay Area Writing Project, established by James Gray at UCLA-Berkley in 1974, and the work and writing of Donald Graves at the University of New Hampshire, who published *Teachers and Children at Work* in 1983.

For three weeks, we began the day in our writing groups, progressed to a three-hour session on writing theory, presented by various experts across the state, and ended the day with time for study, reflection, and writing revision. The emphasis was on writing as a recursive process which cycles through stages of brainstorming, drafting, editing, revising, and publishing. They taught us that we write to communicate and to learn what we know. The cardinal rule is that *Writers write*. There is no substitute for it, and that is why teachers are encouraged to write alongside their students.

I took this back to my classroom the next fall in the form of regularly scheduled writing workshops, where students were allowed to brainstorm, draft, and share their writing through peer editing sessions. Every day, I required students to write in their journals, according to the following rules:

1. Write on the topic of the day or write on your own topic, but you must write something.
2. You may share what you have written but you are not required to do so.
3. All journal writing is confidential, to be read only by the teacher, not for a grade but for affirmation. The only exception is if a student writes something that may be of danger to him or herself or another, the teacher must share it with a parent and/or administrator.
4. If you do not want the teacher to see your writing on a given day, fold the page and staple it together.
5. All journals are kept in a crate in the room and will be returned to the crate after journal time. The journals may be taken home at the end of the year.

We all wrote every day and used our entries to develop pieces of writing which we edited, revised, and published.

I found the writing workshop to be the most inclusive teaching method I had yet encountered. Everyone can participate. Everyone can be successful at his or her own level of competence. There are no *Bluebirds* or *Redbirds*, just a room full of writers seeking to learn, communicate, and collaborate. After my summer at Pembroke, I was invited to join a team of teachers from Cumberland County Schools in planning workshops in *Writing across the Curriculum*, which we conducted with faculties in secondary schools across the district the next year. I enjoyed collaborating with other teachers to develop the content for the workshops and found that I liked working with and presenting to adult learners, who behaved very similarly to my seventh grade students, especially at the end of the day when they were tired and ready to go home.

By the time we left Buie's Creek and moved to Winston-Salem, I was beginning to think about moving from the classroom into the area of supervision or administration. Bill had taken on a new challenge as President of the Homes, which had him traveling all over the state. Our boys were enrolled in three different schools, and were trying to make new friends and get settled into their new environment. It made sense for me to put my teaching career on hold for a while and stay at home. I decided to enroll in a graduate class in supervision at UNC-Greensboro to test the waters regarding my desire to pursue further studies. I would study during the day, prepare dinner, and head out for Greensboro about the time Bill was getting home from work. He would serve dinner, supervise the boys' homework, and get them to bed.

It worked well enough for that first semester, and I decided to apply for the doctoral program in Educational Leadership and attend school full time. I finished most of my course work between spring of 1987 and 1988, attending class three nights a week and taking a full load in summer school. I could not have done it without Bill's help and support, and his willingness to pinch-hit those many hours with the boys.

In January of 1988, I took a job with Winston-Salem/Forsyth County Schools as curriculum coordinator at Wiley Middle School. It was the first year the position had been funded at the middle school level, and I replaced a curriculum coordinator who moved in the middle of the year.

The school system had a superintendent named Zane Eargle, who supported the notion of strong instructional leadership at the building level as the key to improved student learning. He placed curriculum coordinators in all of the schools K-12 for the purpose of assisting the principal and enhancing his/her role as instructional leader of the school. He provided extensive staff development for all of the curriculum coordinators in a train-the-trainer model, and brought in an array of national experts with cutting-edge educational theories to work with us and equip us for our roles.

To mention only a few in-service opportunities, we studied with Howard Johnston on Cooperative Learning, Robert Marzano on Tactics in Thinking, Richard Paul on Lesson Remodeling, Art Costa on Teaching Thinking, and spent three days at the Institute of Government in Chapel Hill learning about the Paideia approach to seminar teaching from the Mortimer Adler Institute. The content and quality of our training could have rivaled the master's programs in curriculum offered in any of the most prestigious graduate schools in education in North Carolina.

The training in curriculum and instruction meshed beautifully with my doctoral courses in Educational Leadership at UNC-G and became the foundation for my dissertation on *Exemplary Middle School Principals*, which I completed in 1991 in fulfillment of the requirements for the doctoral program. It was a naturalistic study of five principals across the state who had been nominated by a panel of middle school experts—e.g., the president and past president of the North Carolina Middle School Association, education professors at UNC-G, a superintendent, etc.—as being among the most exemplary middle school principals in the state.

The birthing of that dissertation was a complicated and frustrating affair, compounded by the fact that I had chosen a committee comprised of professors from both the department of Curriculum and Instruction, as well as from Administration. They rarely saw eye to eye on anything, and put me through endless revisions, which one member would read and mark with changes that virtually took us back to the pre-revised status. When I finally realized that this would go on forever, I told my chair that the writing was done, and that they could take it or leave it. Miraculously, they all signed off on it and complimented me on a job well done. They even nominated it for the annual middle school dissertation award given by the National Association of Supervisors and Administrators (NASSP), and it won.

I received an impressive plaque for it, which was presented in absentia at the NASSP conference in San Francisco in the summer of 1992. I was then invited to publish portions of the dissertation in a juried middle school journal, which I did the following year.

Although I learned a great deal from my course work at UNC-G which has been useful in my practice as an educator, I have to admit that I sometimes question the sanity of devoting almost four years of my life to commuting back and forth to Greensboro, studying, reading, writing, listening, and sitting in class, for the purpose of attaining a certificate that says I can be referred to as *doctor*, or *miz doctor* as some of my students in Lexington used to call me.

There is no doubt in my mind that anybody with average intelligence and the determination of a bulldog can earn a degree. However, one question haunts me to this day: What great things could I have accomplished or what kind of fortune could I have made if I had taken all of those hours and devoted them to another goal?

With my credentials in hand, I entered the market for public school administrators and found that there were way too many candidates in the Winston-Salem Forsyth School system seeking jobs in that area. I was unsuccessful in finding a position in Winston-Salem and took a job twenty miles down the road with Lexington City Schools, home of the best barbeque in the world, and at that time a major furniture town. I was hired as assistant principal of Lexington Middle School and Testing Coordinator for the system, and later became principal there. For seven years, I would leave Winston-Salem with the smell of fresh tobacco in the air from the RJ Reynolds plant, and enter Lexington with the aroma of barbeque cooking at Lexington Barbeque, or the *Honey Monk* as it was affectionately called, after the owner Wayne Monk.

Lexington City Schools is located in Davidson County and is one of a few LEA's in North Carolina that has not merged with the county system. A county seat town, Lexington is a community of great economic disparity. Lawyers, doctors, small business owners, and plant executives live in nicely appointed homes around a country club and in restored homes downtown, while a large community of poor Black and Latino and Southeast Asians, in those days employed in the furniture plants and on construction sites, lived in rented apartments, trailer parks, and in the company houses that were built by the old Erlanger Mill.

The city system was composed of three elementary schools, one intermediate school, a middle school, and a high school. At the time I was there, the enrollment was about sixty percent minority, about half of whom were Black. We also had a large Latino population as well as a number of students from Cambodia and Viet Nam. Our greatest challenge was to meet the needs of our disadvantaged students and at the same time satisfy the demands of the more affluent parents, who, in essence wanted to create a private school within a school for their children.

With the minority populations concentrated in the two city schools, Lexington and Thomasville, the Davidson County School System was about ninety-eight percent white, and the county folks seemed to be okay with that. Lexington and Thomasville were two culturally and racially diverse islands in a white, ultra-conservative sea.

When we took our students to the Davidson County schools to compete in sports, they sometimes encountered an environment which extended beyond one of edgy competitiveness. On more than one occasion, our players were confronted with racial slurs thrown at them by the opposing players. It was certainly not condoned by hosting administrators, but it was sometimes ignored.

However, our students were talented athletes and they learned early that they could keep their *Yellow Jacket Pride* by channeling their superior athleticism into running up the score of the game rather than resorting to street fighting tactics to bloody the nose of a heckler.

It was during those years in Lexington that I realized how much I wanted to be a part of the solution for those middle grades children from backgrounds where poverty and racial and cultural bias impede learning and development. I was convinced that Ron Edmonds was right when he concluded from his Effective Schools Research that we would know that our schools are successful when the children of the poor perform as well as the children of the rich. The theme of leveling the playing field, not by lowering expectations, but by raising them for all children, is one that has resonated with me ever since. That would be something worth working for. That theme would define my work, and I believe it is one that I will continue in my elder season in some form or context.

Politics in a county supporting three school systems sometimes became brutal, sparked by funding issues with the commissioners, the constant talk of merger, and the ongoing dance of the city systems to keep the country club parents happy so that they would not pull their children out and enroll them in a Davidson County school. To complicate matters, the chairman of the board was a micro-manager, who second guessed everything the administrative staff did and insisted that every principal bring his/her year-end teacher evaluations and renewal contracts before the board to be reviewed line by line. The sessions were exhausting and would continue into the wee hours of the night. In most school systems, the principals' recommendations for teacher renewals are a part of the board's consent agenda and are voted on only as a formality.

I found myself in the crossfire when the superintendent who hired me, fell out of favor with said chair. My contract as assistant principal was ready to expire and the principal was on leave for a year to head up a school assistance team for the State Department of Instruction. The superintendent came before the Board and recommended me to take over as principal.

At a meeting that lasted until 1:00 am, the Board not only denied that request but also voted, after two of its members had finally gone home, not even to extend my assistant principal contract. The chair was reputed to have used this late hour tactic on more than one occasion whenever he anticipated a split vote.

I could write a book on the events surrounding that incident, but that is not the purpose of this chapter. Suffice it to say that after the superintendent came to my office on a Friday afternoon in May, to break the bad news that I would no longer have a job with Lexington City Schools, I wandered around all weekend in shock and bewilderment trying to take it all in. By Monday, the news was out, and the hue and outcry that went up protesting my dismissal began, and escalated to the extent that we accomplished very little around the building. When *The Lexington Dispatch* came out on Thursday, the chair of the board had received five *Bricks* in the *Bricks and Bouquets* feature of the editorial page.

Our family flew out to Boston the following Sunday to attend Todd's graduation from Harvard Law School. It was a wonderful diversion that allowed me to forget the crazy world of Lexington City Schools and gain perspective on the situation. We were still in Boston when the Board met that next Monday night. My friend Minnie, who was also the school counselor, faxed the article about the meeting that appeared in next day's *Dispatch* to our hotel room. It seems that the board members were barraged with complaints about their action to fire me and a number of people had signed up to speak publicly on my behalf at the meeting.

The Board went into closed session and watched through the window as a crowd of students and parents and community members queued up outside, with placards and banners, waiting to get in. After some time, the chair went to the door and announced that the Board had voted to re-instate me and that there would be no need for anyone to speak.

The chair of the board was elected as a judge the next fall and had to resign to avoid a conflict of interest. The superintendent retired when his contract ran out at the end of the next year. I stayed on as principal until 1999, when I took the job as principal of East Iredell Middle School, where I worked until my retirement in 2011.

I had been devastated by the initial firing and flattered by all of the attention and support to reinstate me; but, in actuality, I was merely a pawn in an ugly game for control. The chair appeared oblivious to the impact of his actions upon my life and even took the opportunity to tell me how glad he was that I had agreed to stay on.

I had grown to love the students and staff at Lexington Middle School, and was fond of that barbeque town—its unique history and its interesting sites. However, at that point, I felt it was time to look for opportunities to work elsewhere. When I was offered the job in Statesville, I took it.

In many respects, I enjoyed being a principal and was at my best functioning as the instructional leader in the building. But I found some of the supervisory aspects of the job, such as cafeteria and bus duty, to be tedious and downright boring. And, as chief disciplinarian, to sit at my desk and listen endlessly while a pair of seventh grade girls gave their intricate he-said, she-said excuses to justify why they had drawn all over the bathroom walls, or why they had disrupted class for the umpteenth time, was sometimes excruciating. Besides, it made no sense that they were missing valuable instructional time rehearsing their drama in front of me, and would miss even more time, assuming I followed the discipline code to the letter, and assigned them to in-school suspension for the following day.

Had it not been for the dynamic leadership that Terry Holiday brought to the district when he became superintendent in 2002, I would have eventually taken early retirement or found a job slinging hash at a fast food restaurant rather than continue on as a principal.

Dr. Holiday implemented a systems approach that was both systematic and systemic throughout the district, for the purpose of supporting learning for every child K-12. He was not satisfied with what he called pockets of excellence in the district that had been created through random acts of improvement specific to certain schools and classrooms. This set up an institutional *crapshoot,* where students who were lucky enough to draw the good schools and good teachers received the best education.

He insisted that through aligned acts of improvement, we could create a system where every student, regardless of the school he/she attended or the teacher to whom he/she was assigned, could master the skills and knowledge necessary to advance to the next level. The system is built on aligned tiers of leadership that cascade down from the district to the school to the teacher and to the individual student level. Each level of leadership depends upon the one below it to achieve its goals. The classroom depends on the individual students to accomplish its goals, which are aligned with the school goals, which are aligned with the district goals.

The continuous improvement process hinges upon the creation of aligned goals, which are evaluated through a four-step cycle called a PDSA (Plan, Do, Study, Act). The process begins with a plan of action (Plan), moves through the implementation of that plan (Do), followed by the review and study of the outcomes of the plan (Study), and finally the modification and revision of the plan according to evidence from the study phase (Act). The revisions from the Act phase become the new Plan phase, as the process continues and improvements are made. The

PDSA continues until the goal is reached and there are no more improvements to be made.

At that point, the goal is maintained by periodic monitoring and it becomes a standardized process for how the system does business in that area. For example, when the process for improving reading scores among middle grades students has been established, the elements of that same process can be used in establishing a process to improve math scores.

Iredell Statesville Schools made great strides under Dr. Holiday's leadership and in 2008, our system was awarded the prestigious Malcolm Baldridge National Quality Award,[1] the highest Presidential award for organizational innovation and performance excellence. I learned almost as much about effective instructional leadership in the seven years during which he was superintendent as I did in my entire doctoral program.

I had begun looking for a central office position that would allow me to work exclusively in the area of curriculum and instruction even before Dr. Holiday left the system in 2009 to become the Commissioner of Education for the State of Kentucky. It appeared that an opportunity to work as a Middle School Director in Curriculum and Instruction was about to present itself in the spring of 2008, when the recession came along and the budget cutbacks began. Positions at the district level were the first to be cut, and the position promised to me was put on hold. Everybody who still had a job was grateful for it, and I was no exception. The national economic crisis had a way of putting things in perspective and suddenly, my complaints about the more tedious aspects of building level administration seemed petty in the face of all the suffering and job loss going on around me.

As the economy began to recover, funding was partially returned and the position that had been put on hold re-opened. In the interim, there had been a change in leadership at the district level, and the position was offered to a younger candidate. It became evident that the door for growth and further advancement under this administration had been closed to me.

I was coming close to the two benchmarks that would allow me to retire with full benefits from the state and from Social Security—thirty years employment and sixty-six years of age. I knew that my tolerance for remaining a principal was burning out, but there were several exciting initiatives going on in education that I really wanted to hang around for, and I was pretty sure I could do that in a central office setting.

One of those initiatives was the common core curriculum,[2] which I believe will finally bring our schools into the twenty-first century in terms of instruction. The other was a new North Carolina Teacher Evaluation instrument[3] that is infinitely more complex than the old North Carolina Teacher Performance Appraisal Instrument (TPAI) in its measurement of the degree to which teachers are engaging students in twenty-first century learning skills.

I was terribly disappointed not to have the opportunity to fulfill my goal of working in curriculum and instruction and I had difficulty shaking both that disappointment and the resentment I felt at being passed over. I stayed on at East Middle for one last year, to close out some unfinished commitments, and in August of 2011, I ended my thirty-year career. Thanks to the soundness of the North Carolina State Retirement Fund and the generosity of my husband, I was fortunate to be in a position financially to walk away from a situation that was becoming increasingly unsatisfactory.

My mother once told me a true anecdote about a father and son who were both musicians. I should know who they were, but do not remember. The father went to bed early every night and the son often stayed out late. On his return, the son signaled to his father that he was home for the night by going to the piano and playing a familiar melody almost to the end, leaving the last note hanging. He would then switch off the light and go up to bed. He did this to annoy his father, who he knew could not go back to sleep until the piece was finished. Minutes later, the son would hear the light click back on, followed by the sound of his father's footsteps on the stairs, and finally the sound of the last note being struck, bringing resolution to the piece. His father would then pad back up the stairs, turn off the light, and sleep peacefully until morning.

My final experience with Iredell Statesville Schools was a bit like that, except I never had the satisfaction of playing the last note. When I closed my office door and walked out into the sultry summer evening a year ago, I left unfinished a melody that I had been playing for thirty years. I do not know what that means in terms of my future work, but somewhere and somehow, and in some form, I will be looking for a place to strike that last cord and finish the song.

CHAPTER 8

Resolution: *Journey Inward*

The longest journey is the journey inward. Dag Hammarskjold

Reflecting on my Relationship to the Institutional Church

Since I retired, I have begun to rethink my relationship to the institutional church to determine its relevance to my life and to my core beliefs, all part and parcel of the project I undertook this year to deal with the physical and spiritual baggage impeding my journey into the elder season.

As one who was raised a Southern Baptist preacher's kid or *PK* as we were called, I have carried on a love-hate relationship with the institutional church for as far back as I can remember. It was in the arms of the church that I was nurtured and loved and made to feel like a chosen child of God; where I was taught to care about the poor and disenfranchised, to advocate for justice and equality, to spread the gospel of inclusiveness and love in the world, and to read and interpret the scriptures critically and honestly. It was in the church that I learned my Baptist heritage: about the Priesthood of Believers, about local church autonomy, about the ordinance of Believer's Baptism.

It was from the resources of the church and through the generosity of many of our parishioners that our family drew its livelihood, received comfortable housing, and was afforded many of the niceties and luxuries of life. It was in and around the church where I made my friends and passed my time.

And yet, it was because of the church that my life was disrupted and my roots were pulled up over and over again whenever my father would answer a new call and move us to a new town, a new church, and a new school, where we would begin again putting down our roots and making a new start.

My mother was the consummate homemaker, and every time we would move, she would pack a box of sheets and bedspreads and towels and take them with us in the car. When the moving van arrived at the new parsonage, she would insist that the beds be set up and made first thing. She was convinced that the sooner my sister and I were surrounded by familiar things, the sooner it would seem like home and the sooner we would begin to adjust. She made certain that we always spent the first night in our own beds, on our own sheets, snuggled down under our own covers.

My dad was not at all a traditional Baptist preacher and we were never subjected to the fire and brim stone sermons that put many of the more thoughtful preacher's kids of my era on the therapist's couch as adults. He was well educated, liberal, and the antithesis of a biblical literalist. He encouraged us to question our faith and seek the truth wherever we might find it. Nor, was he or mother overly strict in imposing unrealistic rules or morals on us. They allowed us to be normal children and to pursue the activities and interests that any other normal children would.

That was not always the case, however, with some of our parishioners. One of my high school Sunday school teachers, I will call Mr. Cesar, who stood firmly on his belief in scriptural inerrancy, became flustered and annoyed with my repeated interruptions and challenges to the accuracy of his lessons. In his defense, I was an obnoxious little liberal know-it-all, who probably would have annoyed Jesus himself. However, the point is, he looked straight at me and asked: "Do you think that maybe the Devil gets inside of people—oh, I don't know— like minister's children, to undermine the truth and to discredit their father's work?" I told him I did not believe in the Devil, at which point he ended the lesson and led us all in a word of prayer.

I told my dad about it at Sunday dinner and it made him furious. Later on I overheard him say to my mother, "Why that damn little whipper snapper! How dare he say something like that to my child? I ought to break his neck." Several weeks later, Mr. Cesar was transferred to the junior high department and we got a new teacher in the high school class.

Sometimes my dad's independent views could cut the other way and become a source of embarrassment and frustration for me. That was the case when I was eleven and we were living in Siler City. The practice of the women and girls wearing corsages and the men and boys wearing boutonnieres to the Easter Sunday service was a sacred custom there. Usually the women would have an orchid or sometimes a small spray of roses pinned to their dresses, and the men would wear a single carnation or a rose. My dad felt that cut flowers were a waste of money, in that they died so quickly, and thought that the corsages and boutonnieres commercialized and detracted from the real meaning of Resurrection Sunday. I do not think my mother cared about it one way or the other, but in our family there were definitely no flowers worn on Easter Sunday.

As a pre-teen, I was acutely aware of being absolutely the only one among my friends without a corsage and I was humiliated for myself and for my family at being singled out in this way. I am certain that if I had shared these concerns with my mother, she would have seen to it that I never went without flowers again, as she always erred on the side of peoples' feelings over principle, especially the feelings of her children. However, for some reason, I could never give voice to my concerns, and so I suffered in silence, dreading the approach of Easter Sunday for the four years we were in Siler City.

One year, as the sun rose on a brand new Resurrection Sunday, I arose with a high fever and red splotches all over my body. A case of rubella would keep me in bed and home from church and the disgrace of attending Sunday school flowerless. In the lines of the old hymn, *God moves in strange and mysterious ways, his wonders to perform*.

Growing up in a minister's family was an education in and of itself. When we lived in Siler City, the parsonage was next to the church, on highway 421, directly across the road from the city hall. A Gulf station was on the corner, and Buckner's Funeral Home was in the next block. My dad's office was in the house and we never knew who would come by, or at what hour they would show up. It might have been a familiar church member dropping off a freshly baked cake before she went next door to the WMU meeting or a deacon coming by to make a call. Sometimes there were emergencies and the visitor was too distraught to ring the doorbell. Like the time the young woman burst through the front door in the middle of the afternoon calling out "Dr. Poerschke, Dr. Poerschke, help us! Daddy's gone and shot himself."

In addition to our immediate church members, there were a number of interesting characters who made regular stops by our house and who we encountered when we were out and about the town.

In the fifties, there were no separate homes or sheltered workshops provided for mentally or emotionally challenged adults who lived in small towns like Siler City. These folks did the best they could, relying on the goodwill of the community at-large for their sustenance and livelihood.

One of these individuals was Victor, a man in his forties, who was mentally disabled, and had a cleft palate, which impeded his speech. He managed quite cleverly to live independently off the odd jobs around the community and from the food and other donations that he received from the local churches and charitable agencies in town.

Victor was a regular visitor at our house. He would stop by to collect his holiday baskets from the church, to report on the health of various members of his family, or to show us something that he had collected on his daily rounds about town.

One morning, my mother was doing the breakfast dishes, when she heard a knock on the screen door at the back of the house. She stepped from the kitchen out onto the screened porch to see who was there. When she got to the door, she found Victor, standing on the back stoop. He was holding up a giant string bean, pinched between his thumb and index finger.

"Miz Poerschke," he beamed." I jus' wanted to show you this string bean. I grew it myself. Ain't this the wongest fing you ever seen?" Mother had to admit that it was indeed an impressive sight, and she judged that it was at least a foot-and-a-half long, dangling there in Victor's outstretched hand.

Victor was a man of prayer and would never leave our house until he had led us all in a benediction in which he blessed every person, every living creature, and every tree and blade of grass around.

I always made myself scarce when I saw him coming into the front yard, to avoid my pre-teen embarrassment of being caught praying in public; but many was the time he raised his hand over all of us and I failed to get away before he said, "Wet us Pway. OOOOO, Ward, pwease bwess...."

As soon as that happened I was doomed to stand there, head bowed and eyes closed, until Victor would run out of things to bless, conclude with a devout "Amen!" and be on his way. I dared not duck out, for my parents would not have tolerated any act of disrespect toward this man, who despite his limitations, was a child of God and of infinite worth. Nevertheless, I would utter my own silent prayer that I would not be caught in this predicament again, and that none of the cars whizzing by on the highway only twenty feet from our front yard where we were all bowed in prayer, were carrying any of my friends or acquaintances.

My dad loved Victor and developed a good relationship with him. He was aware that Victor's father was terminally ill and had paid him several visits. One day Victor stopped by the house on his way back from spending time with his father, whose condition had worsened and who was now at Chatham County Hospital. My dad was mowing the front yard and called out to Victor to inquire about his father. Victor teared-up and said:

"Diddy's not doing so good, Dr. Poerschke. He's weel sick and I don't fink he's gonna make it much wonger. "

"Victor, I'm so sorry to hear that," my dad responded.

"Ya know, Dr. Poerschke, Diddy asked me to pway for him. He said 'Victa, I know you are a man of God en I want you to pway to God and tell Him to make me well.'"

"En I said, 'Diddy, you know I will pway for ya. But, remember, Diddy. pwayer jus' ain't gonna take the woof off da house!"

That remark blew my father away and you can be sure it was repeated in future lessons and sermons on the real meaning of prayer.

One of my favorite Victor anecdotes was told to us by a friend and church member. She said that Victor and his brother Jack came by her house one day looking for work. She wracked her brain, trying to think of something, and finally hit on a job she thought they could do. She knew that Victor was the brains of the outfit and that Jack would do whatever he was told.

"Okay, Victor," she said. "There is a heavy wooden doll house against the fence in the grassy part of the back yard. The girls have outgrown it, and I will pay you two to move it to the other side of the fence and get it out of the way."

Victor agreed to take the job, and he and Jack set out to move the dollhouse. The back yard formed a large rectangle, with no fencing around the perimeter, but a decorative picket fence bisecting the yard about two-thirds of the way back, where the grass stopped and the ground was bare. There was a gate in the middle of the fence. The dollhouse sat up against the fence near the left side of the gate.

Our friend watched through the kitchen window as Victor and Jack approached the task. The first thing that occurred to them was to slide the dollhouse through the gate. They pushed and pushed, but the gate was clearly too narrow and the house would not go through. They stopped and pondered the situation, not taking into account that they could simply slide the house to end of the fence and around to the other side, there being no fencing around the perimeter. After a few minutes, Victor explained something to Jack, Jack nodded, and the two of them positioned themselves on either side of the dollhouse and began to lift it. Before our friend could get to the kitchen door leading to the back yard and call out the obvious solution, they had lifted the dollhouse over their heads and heaved it over the fence, where it landed upside down, roof first, on the other side.

Incredulous and amazed, our friend stood in the open kitchen door as Victor dusted off his hands and walked toward her.

"Well, Miz Budd," he proudly announced. "Vere's more van one way to skin a cat!"

People like Victor enriched our lives and the lives of the community. I remember him now with great affection; although, at the time, I was unable to appreciate his worth, due to my own insecurity and self-consciousness.

I was at that age where I hated being singled out by adults, especially those with any apparent flaw or idiosyncrasy. It was a simpler time in the mid- fifties, and my parents did not worry much about child abductions and rape and murder. However, they did worry about manners and respect for others; and, I knew that any time an adult spoke to me, I was expected to respond courteously, no matter where I was and how many friends were around.

I was always running into people in the community who knew my father and wanted to be remembered to him when they saw me; and, I understood that as soon as eye contact was made, I was expected to respond politely.

That is why, whenever a group of us would meet up at the Food Liner on our way to school in the morning, to stock up on gum and candy, I would avoid the coffee aisle like the plague.

That was where Adam Blake would usually be. Adam was a veteran who suffered from shell- shock and other injuries while he was in combat during World War II. I don't know if the war was fully or only partially responsible for his condition, but to me, his appearance and manner were ghastly. He was a huge man, with coarse black hair that stood up in all directions. His eyes bulged and his speech was slurred and halting. One of his hands was withered and drawn. He always looked disheveled in his bib overalls and stained work shirts, as he limped along with great effort in his heavy, grease-splattered brogans. He had a wife and two little children but had difficulty supporting them. My dad had served as a chaplain in the Navy during the war and he took a special interest in Mr. Blake and tried to get financial assistance for him through the Veterans Administration.

The manager of the Food Liner paid Mr. Blake a small wage for grinding bags of coffee for the customers. He would stand by the coffee grinder and take orders, and then grind the coffee and deliver it to the customer at the checkout counter. Despite his appearance, he was a gentle, lovable soul, for whom everyone in the community felt sympathy. He absolutely loved my father, and anytime he would spot me, he would bellow my name and begin extolling his virtues.

"Well, hello Miss Poerschke," he would roar, loud enough for everyone in the store to hear.

"I want to tell you that yur Diddy is the finest man I know. He's been so good to me and my fam'ly and hepped us so much. You be sure and tell him I said hello." At that point, he would become emotional and start to sob.

"I just don't know anybody finer 'en him. He is such a good man. You be sure and tell him that Adam Blake said hello. 'Cause, like I said, he done so much for me." Like an old drunk on a binge, he could not stop once he got started on the subject of my father. I would stand there, smile, and nod my head up and down. Finally, when I could get a word in edgewise, I would stammer, "Okay, thank you Mr. Blake. I'll tell him, but I have to go to school now."

I mentioned earlier how much our lives were disrupted when my father and mother decided to pull up roots and move to a new church. The move from Siler City to Jacksonville Florida in 1959, when I was just beginning high school, and the subsequent move to Birmingham, Alabama only a year and a half later, when I was a rising high school junior were especially painful for me.

When my dad accepted the call to Morningside Baptist Church in Jacksonville, he thought he was going there to participate in a bold new venture called a shared ministry, where there would be no traditional *senior minister* primarily responsible for preaching and tending to the more affluent members of the flock. Everyone on the ministerial team would share alike in the duties of preaching, teaching, counseling, and visitation. My dad had advocated that style of ministry for many years, and was anxious to become a part of such a team.

As it turned out, the model of shared ministry did not materialize and my dad discovered that he and the church were ill fitted to one another, forcing him to seek employment elsewhere. The church, formed by members of Riverside Baptist Church, had many issues that it never resolved, and it eventually disbanded.

After several tense months, my dad found a place as Minister of Education at Mountain Brook Baptist Church, which was located in an affluent bedroom community of Birmingham, Alabama. It was a good fit for him in that he had formerly spent ten years in Charlotte as Minister of Education at Myers Park Baptist Church, during which time he was given a leave of absence to pursue a Doctorate in Education from Columbia University in New York City. We lived in Birmingham until I was a junior at Furman, when

Daddy accepted a position to teach in the Religious Education Department at Southeastern Seminary in Wake Forest, North Carolina, where he and mother lived until his retirement.

Mountain Brook Baptist Church had offered our family the use of a spacious two-story home, gifted to the church by a retired couple in the congregation. Daddy was the only one who had seen it before we moved, and he used a bit of reverse psychology in describing it to Mother, by downplaying its desirability. He portrayed the house as old but *adequate,* and assured her that we were not obligated to live there and could find another place later on.

We were all overjoyed with the sight that we encountered when we pulled into the driveway at 66 Overbrook Road for the first time, in a pouring-down June rain. There stood an imposing white colonial, two-storied house with green shutters, and square columns supporting an ample front porch laid in flagstone.

The property had been well-maintained and included a two car garage with a screened-in *summer room* attached to it. In contrast with Daddy's description, the place looked like a mini Mount Vernon. Mother fell in love with it at first sight. Her appreciation for the house grew when she saw how well the interior had been maintained and how perfectly our belongings would fit into it.

My mother, father, sister, and even my grandmother, who had moved in with us after Granddaddy's death, adapted almost immediately to the community and loved it for its charm, beauty and Southern appeal. However, I never really got my roots down in Birmingham. After two moves in less than two years at such a formative stage in my life, I became like a log bobbing along as the current carried me downstream to some future destination waiting around the bend somewhere ahead. It was not until I graduated high school and went off to Furman that I regained my bearings and felt grounded again.

A rising junior in high school, I felt like I had arrived late to the party. My new school, Shades Valley High, had an enrollment of 2500 students. On the first day I attended class there, I did not see one familiar face, even though I had met a number of kids at church over the summer.

The social environment of the peer group into which I was thrust, was sophisticated and privileged. It ran the gamut from high school sororities to holiday parties at the country club, to elaborate travel plans during AEA, which was the equivalent of our high school spring break, and, a debutante season, which began the summer after graduation. I was invited to join in the events and festivities, and I did make an effort to do so; however, I always felt a bit like an outsider.

At that time, the steel industry was still going strong in Birmingham and many of the steel executives lived in Mountain Brook, which in 1961 was listed as having the tenth highest income per capita in the United States. The political climate in Alabama was downright raunchy, and you could cut the racial tension with a knife. Every roadside gift shop displayed the fat, red-faced figurine of a Civil War General carrying a Confederate flag and proclaiming *Forget, Hell !* through clinched teeth. A billboard in Vestavia, on the winding road leading up to the massive statue of Vulcan, announced in bold letters *Impeach Earl Warren* and there were still little wrought iron lawn jockeys at the end of many driveways.

Those were the years when Bull Connor, the Commissioner of Public Safety, turned the hoses and dogs on a group of peaceful Black protesters and children; when Martin Luther King wrote his letters from Birmingham Jail, and the National Guard parked its tanks and guns on the Jefferson County Court House lawn, in Downtown Birmingham.

I saw the tanks firsthand one night when my friend *Beanie* Potts convinced me to skip Wednesday night services at the church and tell our parents that we needed to go home and do our homework.

Instead, the two of us climbed in *Beanie's* Ford Mustang and took the fifteen-minute ride from Mountain Brook into Birmingham to get a look at what was going on, giggling and joking all the way. When we arrived at the Courthouse, the sight sobered us up quickly. It was like turning the corner and suddenly running into an occupied zone, with armed guards, guns, and cannon. Speechlessly, we hightailed it out of there, speeding over Shades Mountain, and back to Mountain Brook in time for *Beanie* to drop me off at my house and get home before our parents returned from church.

When a federal law passed, requiring all public facilities to be open to all races, the pools and public tennis courts were closed in Birmingham, the consensus being that we had rather not swim at all if we have to have mixed race bathing. The wealthy still had the option of swimming and playing tennis at the country club.

At school, we were barraged by assemblies sponsored by John Birchers, warning us of the dangers of Communism and trotting out every poor immigrant who had managed to escape from one of the Communist bloc countries and had a story of persecution and horror to tell.

Many people were building bomb shelters and the schools conducted regular evacuation drills in case we ever had a nuclear attack. John Kennedy was president and he was despised in Alabama almost as much as FDR had been twenty years earlier, but not as much as his brother Robert, whom he had appointed as Attorney General of the United States. George Wallace became Governor of Alabama, and Bear Bryant and his Crimson Tide reigned supreme.

There were a number of courageous citizens who worked behind the scenes in Birmingham and throughout the South, to bring about positive change in our charming but oh, so exclusive and entrenched, Southern order. My dad was one of them.

He joined the first interracial minister's association in Birmingham that met and talked about how they might establish dialogue among the churches to promote racial justice. At one of the meetings, he was moved to hear a Black pastor talk about his terror when he saw one of his own innocent children mowed down with a fire hose at one of the demonstrations.

My dad and other Baptist leaders supported the resolution that Bob Seymour, the pastor at Binkley

Memorial Baptist Church in Chapel Hill wanted to send to Martin Luther King in Birmingham jail. Rising on the floor of the Southern Baptist Convention, Seymour repeated his message to Dr. King: *We who are imprisoned salute you who are free*. The motion was soundly defeated.

I was young and idealistic and took up the cause against racial discrimination with great zeal. I must admit, though, that my passion for racial justice resulted in a great deal more talk than action. I had returned to Birmingham for the summer, after my first year at Furman, and was trying my parents' patience with the sophomoric and pretentious attitude that I had acquired over the short time that I had been away from home. I was feeling particularly indignant about the bigotry and intolerance that I perceived I had come back to in Birmingham, and was spouting off to my parents about how unfair things were. It was, of course, like preaching to the choir, and they grew weary of hearing me pontificate, when what they really thought I should be doing was picking up my clothes, making up my bed, and finding a part time job.

One evening, after I had dominated the dinner conversation with pronouncements on the backwardness and prejudice that I felt existed all over the Deep South, the state of Alabama, the city of Birmingham, and even the leadership at Mountain Brook Baptist Church, my dad broke in and said:

"Kathy, you obviously feel very strongly about racial injustice, and as you know your mother and I share your concern. Maybe it is time for you to follow your conscience and do something really courageous to be a part of the solution to the problem. I understand that a number of college students are joining the Freedom Riders movement and are going to Mississippi this summer to help with voter registration. Your mother and I would certainly support you if you decided to take up a cause like that. You could do that instead of finding a summer job."

My mother's wide eyes and cocked brow betrayed her surprise at what my dad had said, but she recovered quickly and told me that, of course, they would certainly be supportive and proud of whatever I decided to do.

However, there was really no cause for her concern. I was not about to go off to Mississippi to help actual, in-the-flesh Black people. My passion was not concrete and specific, but theoretical and abstract. I had been singing joyfully and with conviction all my life about Jesus loving all the little children of the world—red and yellow, black and white, but in truth, when it came to the Black ones, I did not really know many of them.

All of my life I had attended segregated schools, a segregated church, and segregated public facilities, visiting white-only public bathrooms and drinking from white-only public water fountains. I had ridden on buses with signs directing all *Colored Patrons* to sit at the rear of the bus and restaurants that posted signs saying, *No Colored patrons served here*. Even during my first year at Furman, there were no Black students enrolled, and it would be 1965, my junior year, before Joe Vaughn would become the first African American to be admitted, and that was only as a day student.

I did know some of the maids who worked for my friends and for some of my more affluent relatives. There were people like Clem, who made the most amazing biscuits in the world every day for Aunt Annie Mae down in Jacksonville; and Ora, who could put the best fried chicken and green beans I ever tasted on Aunt Lillian's table. I had heard multiple stories about Texie, the woman who loved and raised my mother when her father lost his fortune in the Depression and my grandmother had to go back to work. However, I never had a close relationship with any person of color. I was not raised by a Black nurse and the closest thing to a Black cook we had was my little German Grandmother whose Kranz Kuchen and crumb cake would rival any homemade biscuit.

I believe that there were many white Southerners like me, who had been taught the lessons of love and inclusion in Sunday school. Even those who had been exposed week after week to the threats of hell fire and damnation from the pulpit knew in their hearts that no just and loving God could condone the kind of discrimination and subjugation of the Black race perpetuated by the Jim Crow Laws that were still being enforced throughout the South.

I am certain that there were also many white Southerners like me, who loved the institutional church and struggled to reconcile its biblical teachings with its failure to act upon those teachings by condemning the unfairness of the current order. And, like me, most of those Southerners had lived in such isolation from the Black community all their lives that they would have been hard pressed to find a Black person they could reach out to.

No, I was not going to Mississippi to join the Freedom Riders in the summer of 1964, because the issues of racial justice and equality were still abstract constructs that stirred my conscience and were the subject of my rhetoric; but they had no concrete names and faces that called me to action.

Conditions would soon begin to change with the passage of the Civil Rights Act of 1964[1], the Voting Rights Act of 1965[2], and the Fair Housing Act of 1968.[3] Gradually, as the schools and neighborhoods and restaurants, and finally a few churches became more fully integrated, I became acquainted with more and more people of color through my work as a teacher and an administrator. These contacts became the names and faces behind my constructs of racial justice and equality on which I was able to take action, albeit not as dramatic as joining the Freedom Riders, but action nonetheless. I have alluded to this in my chapter on work; however, the full story is one that wanders far from the purpose of this chapter, and I will save that for another time.

My ambivalence toward the church in the early years was not so much about how it affected my personal faith and beliefs as to how my life was disrupted as the result of my father's being an employee of it. Later on, as I grew into young adulthood, my personal belief system became more the issue, as I struggled with the inconsistency between the church's teaching and its practice, mostly as it related to social and racial justice.

The relationship between the church and me would become even more complicated when, at the end of my sophomore year at Furman, I fell in love with, and eventually married a man who had been accepted to law school at both Emory, in Atlanta, and Washington University, in St. Louis, and decided at the last minute to enroll at Southeastern Seminary in Wake Forest, where my father was teaching in the Department of Religious Education.

Bill and I were married in the Seminary Chapel in the town of Wake Forest, in December of 1967, after we had graduated from Furman the previous June. I had moved home to live with my parents until the wedding, and was teaching US History, World History and conversational French at Wake Forest High School. For the next fifteen years after he graduated from seminary, Bill served as a pastor in local Baptist churches in Eastern North Carolina and the Piedmont.

As the spouse of a minister, I was once again faced with the disruption of moving from place to place. It was easier as an adult to adjust to the changing environment, but I worried for my children that they would experience the loneliness I had felt when I was their age every time I had to meet new people and make new friends. I also chafed under our lack of privacy and the constant watch of our parishioners who took an interest in knowing every detail of our lives.

Sometimes it felt like we were living in a fish bowl, especially during those years in Mount Gilead where the parsonage was right next to the church on Main Street, as well as diagonally across from the only pharmacy and one of the two grocery stores in town. A few of our church members became experts at reading and interpreting the signs of movement around our house, like the one who greeted me at the Sunday service by saying, "Y'all must have really slept in yesterday. When I drove by your house Saturday afternoon, the *Charlotte Observer* was still lying at the end of the driveway." That comment rankled. Not only were our sleeping habits none of his business, but as we had four children under the age of six living in that modest ranch style parsonage, our chances of sleeping in were slim to none.

For the most part, those fifteen years were happy and fulfilling, and I would not trade them even if I could. Bill was a diligent and highly effective pastor, and through his work, we became intimately involved with many wonderful church and community people across the eastern part of the state and the Piedmont. They took us into their homes and into their lives, and became our lifelong friends. They reached out to our children and served as an extended family to them in creating a safe, loving, and nurturing environment in which to grow up.

In contrast to the relatively inclusive and harmonious atmosphere of daily life within the sphere of the local church, the atmosphere within the wider sphere of the Southern Baptist denomination grew more divisive and toxic in the late seventies and early eighties. Fanned by the national political climate, which had become ever more right wing and conservative, the tension between fundamentalist and moderate Baptists turned into a virtual holy war.

It was led by clergy and seminary professors and prominent lay people who were staunch biblical literalists determined to purge the denomination of the liberal practices that some of its churches were promoting in the name of inclusion: ordination of women; accepting for church membership those who had been baptized by modes other than immersion; the welcoming of gays and lesbians into the fellowship; the public support of a woman's right to choose abortion over carrying a baby to full term; and, good Lord, don't forget the issue of school prayer! [4]

The battle played out on the floor of the annual meeting of the Southern Baptist Convention, which is an organization through which local Baptist churches have loosely aligned, since 1845, for the common funding and support of missions and seminaries and various agencies.

The messengers representing their local churches, convene yearly to elect a president and other officers, to determine the programs, policies and budget of the convention, and to worship together. The president receives broad powers to appoint committees, which govern and control the agencies, including the seminaries.

The architects for what has come to be known by moderate Baptists as the *fundamentalist takeover*, and by fundamentalists as the *conservative resurgence*, were Judge Paul Pressler[5], an appellate judge from Houston, Texas, and Reverend Paige Patterson[6], at that time a doctoral student at New Orleans Baptist Seminary. In response to what they considered a leftward shift in Convention leadership during the 1960's and early 1970's, they met in New Orleans in 1967 to devise a plan for fundamentalist domination of the Southern Baptist Convention through the election of a president a sufficient number of times to gain a fundamentalist majority on the boards and agencies of the Convention.

In 1979, they organized a get-out-the-vote campaign in fifteen states and bussed a massive number of messengers to the convention in time to vote for president, after which they were bussed back home. As a result, fundamentalist pastor Adrian Rogers was elected president.

Bill and other like-minded pastors and moderate leaders in North Carolina had realized early on the implications of that election in 1979, and had begun to inform and educate their churches as to the repressive changes it would ultimately bring about in denominational institutions and relationships. North Carolina was considered a liberal bastion by many fundamentalist Baptists, and Southeastern Seminary, which was known for its emphasis on critical biblical scholarship and its support of the role of women in ministry, would become a prime target in the takeover.

For years, Baptists, at least in North Carolina, had squabbled and fought among themselves whenever they convened to conduct business for the common cause. Issues of church polity, of who and who would not be accepted for church membership, and of the authority of scripture and how it was to be interpreted in daily action were always loudly and passionately debated through the resolutions that were proposed and either defeated or passed on the floor. The tent was big enough to hold this diverse gathering and the time was taken to hear every conceivable view and perspective. But when the final vote was cast and the majority decision was determined, the messengers would sing a hymn, pronounce a benediction, and return to their local churches to do their part to bring about the Kingdom of God on earth, dictated by their own faith and personal relationship with the Almighty.

In 1985, I witnessed firsthand how the big tent model of Baptist unity from diversity would be unalterably changed. That year, Bill and I took our four boys and drove out to Dallas, Texas to attend the Southern Baptist Convention, as messengers of Memorial Baptist Church, in Buie's Creek. Our family was too large to travel comfortably in either of the two compact cars that we owned, and so Bill rented a large Oldsmobile with bench seats in the front and back, that the boys affectionately dubbed *The Brown Rat*, to get us there. My mother and daddy attended as messengers from Pullen Baptist Church in Raleigh, and My Uncle Schaefer and Aunt Mary were there representing the First Baptist Church in Greenville, South Carolina. We all stayed in the same hotel along with a host of North Carolinians who had come to lend our support to the moderate cause as well as to Southeastern Seminary, and to elect a moderate president.

From the first day, it was evident that the odds were stacked against us. Discussion was strictly monitored and dissent was stifled by cutting off the microphones of those who rose to speak against the fundamentalist agenda. Charles Stanley, fundamentalist pastor at First Baptist Church of Atlanta, was the president and moderator. The auditorium did not fill up until the last day when the slate of officers was voted upon; and, then the buses poured in, the crowds swelled, and the facility was packed with messengers who had been brought in for the sole purpose of winning the vote for the fundamentalists.

A convention that had in past years been conducted by democratic process and in strict accordance to *Roberts Rules of Order*, had become an arena of intolerance. The agenda of the right was enforced, regardless of the toll it took on the freedom of religious expression that had once been the glue binding the disparate group of messengers together in Christian fellowship. The moderates were enraged by the tactics and protested loudly. Stanley, who was visibly shaken by the turmoil and dissent, could do little else but bang his gavel and call order to the session.

By a narrow vote, he was re-elected and the presidency remained for the seventh year in the hands of Judge Pressler and Paige Patterson and their followers. It has never been held by a moderate Baptist since. Ironically, in 2012, Dr. Fred Luter was elected the first Black president of the Southern Baptist Convention. Almost fifty years after the legislation that struck the final blows to the Jim Crow Laws, right wing Baptists have decided to open the door and admit Black men into the circle of convention leadership.[7]

When the Convention mercifully ended, Bill and I licked our wounds all the way back to North Carolina and vowed never again to participate in anything so hopeless and demoralizing. We clearly saw the handwriting on the wall and understood that our denomination would no longer accommodate our beliefs under its tent. In time, the Board of Trustees at Southeastern Seminary was completely replaced with fundamentalists. They did not stop until the president, Randall Lolley, and the entire liberal-minded faculty had either resigned or retired.

Others stayed on to seek reconciliation within the denomination, and many sought new affiliations through the Alliance of Baptists and the Cooperative Baptist Fellowship.[8]

In 1985, Bill left the local pastorate and became president of Baptist Retirement Homes of North Carolina, Incorporated, where he directed his energies toward providing care and services for aging adults. We moved to Winston-Salem and I began in earnest to prepare for a career in public school administration, where I found an outlet for service in working to provide quality education for all of my students, regardless of their gender, race, or culture.

We joined First Baptist Church in Winston-Salem and supported our children as they became integrally involved in the youth program. However, we never did a very good job of connecting with the adult programs there. After the boys graduated, we decided to move our membership to Knollwood Baptist Church. However, neither of us could ever build up a head of steam to become involved there either, and we never gave it a chance.

We buried ourselves deeper and deeper in our respective careers, which we found rewarding and satisfying. I was commuting of outside the community during the week, and I cherished time on Sundays to reflect and plan for the week ahead. Bill traveled extensively during the week and accepted engagements to speak in local churches across the state on many Sundays as well.

Before we moved to Winston-Salem, I had been involved in the life of a local church continuously for as far back as my memory extends. After we moved, I became a virtual church dropout.

It was through my career as a teacher and later an administrator, rather than through the institutional church, that I began attaching names and faces to the abstract constructs of justice and equality that stirred my conscience back in 1964 and made me restless to do something about it. Back then, in my segregated world, I would not have considered the type of activism that might put me on a bus to Mississippi to challenge the status quo there. But as I worked in schools with large minority enrollments and high rates of poverty and disadvantage, I witnessed firsthand the injustice and inequality that tilted the playing field for these students. I learned their faces and their names, and though it was too late to march off to Mississippi on their behalf, I was determined to do anything in my power to level that playing field for them.

Now that I am retired, I have thought long and hard about my relationship to the institutional church from which I have distanced myself for so many years. I feel compelled to understand the history of that relationship and to resolve some of the issues of the past that caused me to turn from it. As I expected, it has been a painful exercise to reflect upon and chronicle my history with the church, especially that period during the fundamentalist takeover of the Southern Baptist Convention, which I have previously described. In fact, I had suppressed it all to the degree that I had difficulty calling back to memory many of the details and dates as well as sequences of events during that time, and was forced to do some fact checking to make sure of the accuracy of my writing.

In the end, I consider the exercise to be a beneficial one. After all, it was in the arms of the church that I first learned about the unconditional love of God and of my responsibility to further His Kingdom on earth. It was in Sunday school where I sang about Jesus loving *all the little children of the world*, and received instruction on the meaning of the words of John to *Know the truth and the truth will set you free*, and those of the prophet Micah to *Do justice, love kindness, and walk humbly with God*. I learned as well that the church did not always live up to its teachings. As I grow older and wiser and have time to reflect upon it, I can only conclude that perhaps it is due to the fact that the church has always been made up of imperfect people just like me.

In time, I hope to be able to better articulate the relevance of the church to my life and to the world. At this point, I am taking baby steps toward reconnecting to it by joining the Faith in Action Sunday school class at Knollwood , and if that goes well, in the fall I will volunteer to help out in one of the intermediate children's Sunday school classes.

Postscript

Shortly after writing this chapter, I had the opportunity to hear Phyllis Tickle speak about her recent book, *The Great Emergence,* and then preach at Knollwood. Tickle is the founding editor of the Religion Department of Publishers Weekly and has become an expert on religion in America, having studied and written extensively about Emergence Christianity in North America. Tickle has an amazing grasp of the events and forces that have shaped Christianity since its birth in the first century, and she summarizes the major upheavals and changes over the past two millennia with clarity and economy, in the first few chapters of the book, which is worth reading, if only to get a good history lesson.

Her spoken words as well as the content in *The Great Emergence* provided for me a context or backdrop for everything I had been writing; and, as I listened to her speak and read her words, things began to take on a new meaning. I made the connection that the experiences and events that I had struggled to recount were all a part of a larger story of a culture, and more specifically a Christianity in the midst of radical transformation.

The thesis of the book is that about every five hundred years the Church goes through a major upheaval, or hinge time, during which its current structures become *an intolerable carapace that must be shattered in order that renewal and new growth may occur.*[9] Tickle compares this phenomenon to a giant rummage sale in which all the old and outmoded trappings of the faith are discarded to make room for newer and more updated furnishings. She explains further that during hinge times, the cable of meaning that keeps society connected to a higher purpose and power, like a small boat tethered to a distant dock, becomes irreparably damaged so that the three strands of rope (representing spirituality, corporeality, and morality) braided together to give strength to the cable, must be rewoven altogether.

From these upheavals, two new entities emerge, the first being a more vital form of the old order, and the second being a new one altogether. For example, the last upheaval was the Great Reformation, which not only brought about a new way of looking at Christianity through Protestantism, but also forced Roman Catholicism to change and become more dynamic. Tickle notes that every time the shell of the dominant version of Christianity is broken open, the faith has *spread dramatically into new geographic and demographic areas, thereby increasing exponentially the range and depth of Christianity's reach as a result of its time of unease and distress.*[10]

Five hundred years before the Great Reformation, was the Great Schism, in 1054, in which the Church split over the *filioque*, or the question of from whence comes the Holy Spirit, resulting in Greek Orthodoxy being practiced in the East, and Roman Catholicism in the West. Five hundred years before that, as the Roman Empire crumbled and lost its hold, Gregory the Great who became pope in 590 CE, led Christianity into a monasticism that would preserve its writing and teachings during the Dark Ages. And, five hundred years before Gregory, in the first century, came the birth of Christianity.

As a phenomenon, the Great Emergence affects all aspects of our twenty-first century lives, from our feelings about information overload to the breakdown of national borders and loyalties; however, it is religion, and more specifically the Christian Religion in North America as it relates to the Great Emergence, that Tickle addresses in this book. Other institutions and world religions as well as other Christians outside of North America have experienced this same cycle of reformation and change; however, Tickle's research and writing focus only on that change as it has manifest itself in North American Christianity.

During a hinge time, the question that must be ultimately answered by the new and emergent form of

Christianity is *Where now is our authority?* For the Great Reformation, the final authority became the scriptures, *Scriptura sola, sola Scriptura* and the priesthood of believers.

The date for the beginning of the Great Reformation is usually considered to be 1517, when Martin Luther nailed his Ninety-Five Theses to the door of Whittenburg Church; but that date is a mere placeholder for convenient reference, *a useful handle that spreads out on either side thereof like a square parcel being carried by a single strap.*[11] Characteristic of the times of upheaval that preceded the Great Reformation as well as those that would follow it, the movement emerged from and was shaped by the political and social and cultural events leading up to it and extending beyond it.

The papal struggles of the late fourteenth and early fifteenth centuries, resulting in the election of two popes, had undermined the primacy and absolute authority of the pope, paving the way to the principle of *Scriptura sola, sola Scriptura* and the concept of the priesthood of believers. But if one were to interpret the scriptures, one had to be able to read them. Wycliffe's translations into the common tongue and Guttenberg's moveable type press that would mass-produce printed materials made that task possible. Universal literacy became a Protestant imperative *and that in turn accelerated the drive toward rationalism and from there to Enlightenment and from there straight into the science and technology and literature and governments that characterize our lives today.* [12]

Likewise, the current upheaval, which Tickle and others refer to generally as the *Great Emergence*, or more specifically, *Emergence Christianity*, has its roots in the challenges to religious authority from the field of science, that began in the mid and late twentieth century, with the publication of Darwin's *The Origin of Species* in 1859 and Faraday's work on field theory. As these theories from the sciences of biology and physics seeped into religious conversation, the Protestant world was thrust into debate over evolution and biblical criticism, and lines were drawn in the sand between what came to be known as Fundamentalist and liberal Protestantism. One of these lines was established at the Conference of Conservative Protestants held in Niagara Falls in 1895, where five principles of doctrine were agreed upon as fundamental to true Christian belief: *inerrancy of the scripture, divinity of Jesus Christ, historicity of the virgin birth; substitutionary nature of Atonement, and the physical, bodily return of Christ.*[13]

The Great Emergence was further influenced by Sigmund Freud's work which explored the conscious and unconscious mind, and Carl Jung, who spoke of a collective unconscious and profoundly influenced later thinkers such as Joseph Campbell, who used the new medium of radio and later television to dispel the Christian doctrines of *particularity* and *exclusivity*, which supported the claim of *solus Christus*, that the only access to salvation is through Jesus. As earlier theories were built upon and sub disciplines and research in such areas as artificial intelligence emerged under the new label of cognitive science, the old answers about self and humanness represented in Descartes premise that *I think, therefore I am*, were becoming insufficient.

Just as the printing press was pivotal to the Great Reformation and its doctrine of *sola Scriptura* and the priesthood of believers, the ever expanding technologies of telegraph, telephone, the automobile, radio, television, and the internet have mobilized and spread the seeds of Emergence Christianity.

Tickle does not believe that we can attach any one date or tell any single story that defines the exact beginning of the Great Emergence. However, in the writings of religious scholars and historians of the twentieth century, we can trace its emergence. It was

Walter Rauschenbusch, in 1907, who wrote, *Western humanity was in the midst of a revolutionary epoch fully as thorough as that of the Renaissance and Reformation.* Rauschenbusch predicted approaching crisis for the church as well as the society in which it existed.[14] Paul Tillich at midcentury began to talk about shifting times and shifting foundations.[15] World War II was over, Hiroshima and the Holocaust had happened, and so had Korea and the Berlin Wall. And then came Vietnam, the Drug Age and Jesus Freaks.

By the late 1960's theologians and historians were speaking of a new paradigm for American Christianity that they illustrated in a diagram called a *quadrilateral*[16] into which all existing forms of American Christians would fall. *Liturgicals* were placed in the upper left quadrant and included Roman Catholic, Lutheran, Anglican, and Eastern Orthodox churches. *Social Justice Christians*, who were originally referred to as *Mainline Christians*, were placed in the upper right quadrant. *Renewalists*, who included Charismatic and Pentecostal Christians, fell into the lower left quadrant. *Conservatives* included Evangelical and Fundamentalist Christians, and fell into the bottom right quadrant.

It is not yet clear what new authority will replace the Protestant principles of *Scriptura sola* and *sola*

Scriptura, and priesthood of believers; however, Tickle believes that it will be some form or fusion of the now differing views on the source of authority, held by two basic groups of North American Christians. One group, which includes both Social Justice and Conservative Christians, which Tickle places on the right side of a quadrant, are convinced that the scriptures are the source from which all authority flows. The other group, which includes Liturgical Christians and Renewalists, which fall on the left side, are not ready to confine God to a fixed set of words and believe in the authority of the Holy Spirit, both through direct inspiration and filtered through the apostolic thinking of those who have been called and ordained.

Also related to the question of authority is that of how one discerns truth. Among the four traditional groups in the quadrant, North American Christians fell into those who subscribed to orthopraxy, right practice, or orthodoxy, right doctrine. With Emergence Christianity, a middle group has formed that could be divided into those who subscribe to Orthonomy, the belief in correct beauty or correct harmoniousness, similar to the Keatsian theory that truth is beauty and beauty is truth, or those who subscribe to Theonomy, the belief that only God is the source of truth.

One characteristic of emergence Christians is that they own no allegiance to the views of a single denomination or quadrant, but have gathered bits and pieces from the four corners, as they participated in the swapping back and forth of information at the water cooler and from other sources made available in an age of media and the internet.

Based on the tendency of past hinge movements to reflect the emerging political and social structures of the time, Tickle predicts that the new authority for Emergence Christianity will be Scripture and the Community, in which the Church will become not so much a thing or an entity, as a network, similar to the World Wide Web. The emergence Church will be *a self-organizing system of relations...between innumerable member parts that themselves form subsets of relations within their smaller networks, etc., etc. in interlacing levels of complexity.*[17]

In such a system, no one member possesses the whole truth. Tickle explains, *The duty, the challenge, the joy and excitement of the Church and for the Christians who compose her, then, is in discovering what it means to believe that the kingdom of God is within one and in understanding that one is thereby a pulsating, vibrating bit in a much grander network. Neither established human authority nor scholarly or priestly discernment alone can lead, because, being human, both are trapped in space/time and thereby prevented from a perspective of total understanding. Rather, it is how the message runs back and forth, over and about the hubs of the network, that it is tried and amended and tempered into wisdom and right action for affecting the Father's will.* The Emergence Church, thus becomes a *conversation.*

It is a movement whose ecclesial authority *waits upon the Spirit and rests in the interlacing lives of Bible-listening, Bible-honoring believers.* It has received some of its impetus from the Great secular Emergence surrounding it, but its tools and theories have been derived from the quadrants, and in one non-quadrant group, which Tickle identifies as Quakers. For in Quaker thought, one does not refuse to engage in the question of authority, but *chooses rather to assume that quiet engagement with God and the faithful reveals authority from the center out to other centers of engagement.* It is that Quaker stance that describes and approximates what Emergence Christianity will ultimately give to the question *What now is our authority?*[19]

CHAPTER 9

Resolution:

Read, Read, Read

*Anyone who says they have only one life to live
must not know how to read a book.*

Author Unknown

Beach Reading

June is the month when our entire family spends one glorious week together at Wrightsville Beach. We have done it for years, ever since our four boys were little, and have continued the tradition as our family has expanded from six to the current total of fifteen and counting. Our beach ritual pastimes include lots of talking and laughing and hanging out together in the water and in the sun, beach walks, early-morning fitness runs for the health conscious, board games at night that become increasingly competitive and edgy as the spirits continue to flow and the hour grows late, and a ton of good eating.

When we come in out of the sun at lunchtime, nothing tastes better than sandwiches made of white bread, slathered with pimento cheese or chicken salad from Robert's Grocery and topped with a thick slice of summer tomato. Nothing is more enjoyable than to gather around the table at night to feast on Bill's fresh flounder cooked on the grill and the peel-your-own shrimp boiled in beer and served with cocktail sauce generously spiked with Texas Pete. The beach affords us seven days of fun and relaxation, with a little bit of family drama mixed in as the week progresses and each person reaches his/her respective level of tolerance for family togetherness.

One of the four brothers usually introduces the off-color pun or double entendre of the week and the game is on to see who can use it the most frequently in casual conversation and in the most suggestive way. Last year, as Harry was mixing up a pitcher of Bloody Marys, he and John started talking about how everyone likes their *BM's*, and the responses got raunchier and raunchier.

I am much more audience than participant in the word play competition. However, one beach ritual that fully engages me is that of reading the selected beach book of the week from cover to cover. I choose that book from those that one of my children recommends, or from the newly published works of favorite Southern authors.

A top favorite selection was Pat Conroy's *Beach Music*, which we all read in summer of 2002, shortly after its publication. Another year, it was the latest Grisham book that held my interest. In 2007, the year that *Harry Potter and the Deathly Hallows* came out, Todd and I sequestered ourselves in our respective rockers and raced to find out whether Harry would kill Valdemort or Valdemort would kill Harry. In summer of 2010, I was reading a gripping book called *The Last Child* by John Hart, an author who grew up in Rowan County, and one that Harry had discovered and passed on to me. It was the year when we all came down with stomach flu. I was waiting my turn for it to hit, praying it would not, but feeling a queasiness that I could not deny. It was a race against time to finish the book before the bug finished me, but I just made it.

This year, the book that topped the charts and left me spellbound was George R.R. Martin's *A Storm of Swords: A Song of Ice and Fire*, the third of five epic fantasy novels already published, with a sixth and seventh in the planning stages. The popular HBO television production *Game of Thrones* is based on the first and second book in the series. After our son Robert kept raving about the show, Bill and I went on a television marathon one weekend and watched all of the episodes of the first season on DVD, and then kept up with the second season episode by episode.

In typical HBO fashion, the shows were edgy, violent, and sexually explicit. I became accustomed to watching the battle scenes with my hands over my face, opening my fingers just a crack to see when it was safe to watch again. Once or twice, we had to fast forward through a scene that simply crossed the line between sexually explicit and pornographic.

Our son Todd also watched *Game of Thrones*, but had already read all five of the *Song of Ice and Fire* books before viewing the television version. He kept urging me to read them; and, when the second season of *Game of Thrones* ended, I became desperate to find out if Tyrion Lanister had been mortally wounded or if he would live on to return in season three. I began a reading binge and finished two of the books before the beach, and once there, I read book three.

The novels are inspired by medieval history, a time that has always captured my interest and imagination. Only recently, I had read several of Phillipa Gregory's historical fictional books based on the struggle between the Lancasters and Yorks in the War of Roses. I had also read Margaret George's novel based on the life of Elizabeth I, as well as Kate Mosse's intriguing thriller *Labyrinth*, set in the Languedoc of southern France at the time of the Albegensian Crusade against the Cathars who inhabited the region. These aspects of the Middle Ages, as well as earlier ones such as the Hundred Years War and the early crusades, were all suggested in the themes and setting of the Martin epic.

Whereas the destiny and fate of the characters in the historical novels aforementioned were pre-determined by the actual events on which the authors based them, Martin's characters do not operate under that restraint. Their conflicts and struggles are played out not only in the fictional Seven Kingdoms of Westeros, but across two fictional continents and within the context of a fictional culture and centuries-long history uniquely created by Martin's imagination. *Songs of Ice and Fire* is an epic story of epic proportion, fantasy, and genius. It is also an astounding display of writer's craft.

I have read that Martin wanted to depict the gritty and brutal reality of medieval life juxtaposed to themes of chivalry and honor that were also characteristic of the time. He has certainly achieved that goal through the creation of a complex and multi-faceted cast of major and minor characters who live and die subject to the blind eyes of fate, with no regard to their importance to the plot. At the end of the first book, two of the major characters had been killed off, and that was only a harbinger of things to come in book three.[1]

I finished *Storm of Swords* and then started on *A Feast for Crows*, book four. That is where I am at the writing of this chapter. You had better believe I will finish book five, *A Dance with* Dragons, before the start of season three of Game of Thrones in March 2013, and go on to books six and seven as soon as they hit the press.

In my pre-retirement days, the professional reading and paperwork that I was required to complete left little time for pleasure reading or reading for personal edification. I have never acquired the skill of speed-reading and my short-term memory is like a sieve, a condition that does not improve with age. Any book I would start would sit partially completed for months and when I would finally pick it up again, I could not remember many of the details and facts previously covered. I had to be content with listening to audio books on the forty-minute daily commute to and from Statesville. It was an ideal way to fill dead time, and I listened only to unabridged editions to make certain that nothing was edited, but it was no substitute for curling up with the book itself and reading it. I suppose that is why the opportunity for sustained reading for one entire week at the beach each year held such an appeal.

Now, I have the luxury of wandering into the land of literature any time I please. It is one of the sheer pleasures that brings joy and enrichment to my life, and one I plan to take with me into my elder season. What could be nicer than beach reading all year long?

Beach Reading All Year Long

I kept my resolution to read frequently and to maintain a record of what I had read. As I trace my journey through the first year of retirement, the list of books is like a trail of breadcrumbs revealing the multiple paths I have taken and interests I have pursued. I have included titles and brief annotations in the following section.

Books for travel that went along to the UK

Rick Steves' Great Britain In 2011 by Rick Steves

The guru of travel, Rick Steves has always been my guide since my very first trip abroad to Italy in 2001. I swear by his advice about restaurants, lodging, and best tourist attractions, although my kids are not as convinced. John only consulted him as a last resort, when he was tired of looking for a restaurant in Venice and snapped, "Give me that damn Rick Dick book and maybe I can find us a decent place to eat."

King Richard III by Shakespeare

This was pre-reading for going to see Kevin Spacey play *Richard III*, at the Old Vic in London, and it helped a great deal in keeping me oriented to the details of the play.

The Pilgrim's Progress From This World To That Which Is To Come by John Bunyan

After Robert and I traipsed all over Bloomsbury to find the statue of John Bunyan for Bill, I felt I should read this.

The Greater Journey by David McCullough

I had read McCullough's books on Truman and John Adams, and picked this one up to read on the plane. It is about the influx of famous Americans studying in Paris between 1830 and 1900, in the fields of medicine, art, music, education, and literature. Samuel Morse, James Fenimore Cooper, Elizabeth Blackwell, John Singer Sargeant, Charles Sumner to mention only a few, found in Paris a place to broaden themselves culturally and educationally, in ways that were not available to them at home.

Books about Sorrow and Loss
Good Grief: 50ᵗʰ Anniversary Edition by Granger E. West

I remembered *Good Grief* (originally published in 1961) as a book that Bill would frequently give to church members who were struggling with loss. It is a very short and simple one that clearly outlines the stages one goes through after the death of a loved one or in response to any major life change. I found it helpful to review as I was uncovering some of my unresolved grief over my father's death and as our family faced the loss of our brother David. I was also interested to see if there was any bereavement literature that would add to or update the notion of *grief work* or stages of grief. I found that in *The Other Side of Sadness*.

The Other Side Of Sadness: What The New Science of Bereavement Tells Us About Life After Loss by George A. Bonanno

A professor of clinical psychology at Columbia University, the author has conducted extensive research on how people experienced loss and what their grief was like. From the stories of the people he interviewed, he concluded that humans are hardwired with an amazing resilience to rebound from the loss and trauma that is an inevitable part of life. The notion of resilience is a departure from the traditional literature on grief and bereavement, which Bonanno claims is narrow in its focus, in that it is written by medical practitioners and therapists who see only people who are consumed by their suffering and need therapy to survive from it.

Bonanno found that most people do not experience grief and trauma in such an overwhelming manner. In the hundreds of stories he heard and recorded, he found no evidence to support the traditional view of a bereavement process demanding what Freud termed *Grief work*. Nor did he find that his subjects experienced the grueling completion of the five stages of grief as a pattern of adjustment after loss—denial, anger, bargaining, depression, and acceptance—which had been a part of the conventional wisdom on grief and loss since Elizabeth Kubler-Ross popularized it in 1969, in her book *On Death and Dying*. Rather, he found that most people, though they felt deep sadness, were able to process their loss and resume their work and other meaningful activities even in the early months after the trauma or death occurred. They were able to experience periods of joy and even laughter, which served as a respite from the sadness.

There was a familiar ring for me in Bonano's scientific notion of human resilience as a response to loss. It was similar to that which I heard in Robert Raines' *A Time To Live*, to which I have already referred, when he spoke, poetically and spiritually, of *spreading our wings in the valley of sorrow* and of weaving the threads of joy and sorrow into a rich and textured tapestry of life.

Saying Goodbye to Your Grief by Hardy Clemons

      I found this tiny book in my dad's library. Hardy Clemons was pastor of First Baptist Church in Greenville, SC, the church that my grandmother and my mother attended, and in which both were married. He was also a good friend to my mother and dad in their Southeastern Seminary days, in Wake Forest. It was written two years after my mother's death and inscribed to my dad: *Bob, my teacher, my friend, and my colleague—I loved Katherine and I love you.*

      In writing about grief from the perspective of an experienced pastor who has ministered to numerous parishioners in their times of loss, Clemons' central message is that every person's response to loss is unique and that every person's time frame for saying goodbye to grief is individual. How long does it take to grieve? *Long enough to focus on the gift more than the loss...grateful for what you lost, hopeful in your new beginning.*[2]

Self-help Books

It's All Too Much by Peter Walsh

The book I used to guide me through the *de-cluttering* process in my house. It is a great resource for anyone needing a systematic plan of attack for cleaning and organizing his/her space and for getting control of our *things* rather than allowing our *things* to control us.

The Happiness Project by Gretchen Rubin

This book gave me the inspiration for my Retirement Project and for the idea of blogging and writing about my journey to find meaning and fulfillment in the elder passage.

The Skinny: On Losing Weight without Being Hungry by Louis J. Aronne

Louis Aronne is a specialist on the problem of obesity and was the doctor who discovered David Letterman's heart condition that led to his heart bypass. The book describes the chemical reaction of hunger in both fat and skinny people. It explains how the presence or absence of certain hormones account for why skinny people feel full and stop eating and fat people never feel full and continue eating. His weight loss plan is sensible and fairly easy to follow. It is built on eating regular meals and snacks, on starting the day with a high protein food such as eggs or a high protein shake, and eating foods that fill you up first, like a soup appetizer or green salad. It is realistic about desserts and foods with empty calories, and does not forbid any food. However, Aronne advises that if you are going to have that piece of candy, eat it after you have had a satisfying meal.

Books for Personal Growth and Awareness
Greedy Bastards by Dylan Ratigan

Ratigan is on a mission to expose the *Greedy Bastards* and *Vampire Industries* that have led to an economic crisis in which the wealthy are getting wealthier, the poor are getting poorer, and the establishment of a permanent underclass in America is a real threat. *If you open your eyes, you will see ordinary, hardworking people struggling. Not far away, you'll find a few greedy bastards making out like bandits, he writes.*[3]

Ratigan defines greedy bastards as those who do not create value for others, but as those who *rig the game so that they can get rich by stealing from the rest of us.* He believes in capitalism and in making money, but what greedy bastards do is not an example of capitalism, but the opposite. Ratigan calls it *Extractionism. It is taking money from others without creating anything of value, anything that produces economic growth or improves our lives.* Ratigan adds frankly, *such people are commonly known as thieves.*[4]

For example, a person who becomes rich from investing in medicine that cures people is one who makes. However, he goes on to say, *If I lobby for changes in a government regulation that helps me trick the union into putting investment funds in flawed investments so that I can collect the commissions, I move as much money into my account as the one who 'makes.' However, I have not made anything. I am a capitalist who takes, exploiting my power to influence government for my private gain.*[5]

The US is a victim of what Ratigan calls Vampire Industries, which prey on the customers instead of trying to provide the highest quality product to serve the customer best. Rewards do not go to who competes best but who cheats best. The solution that the national political parties have offered thus far is like a family bringing the victim to the emergency room. The Democrats want transfusions for the patient, while the Republicans want more guards at the door. Everybody argues about how to stop the bleeding and pain. Pain and bleeding are only the side effects. The cause is the vampire industries.

Ratigan identifies these industries as Banking, Trade, Health Care, Education, Politics, and Energy, and he devotes a chapter each to describing the specific ways in which each is consuming our resources in bad deals made in secret and in disregard for the common good.

The status quo is highly profitable for greedy bastards and they will do whatever they can to prevent new solutions. However, Ratigan believes that we can get at the root problem of breaking the grip of the vampire industries and restore American prosperity, not with silver bullets or silver crucifixes, but with four weapons he calls VICI:[6]

Visibility

Integrity of prices, so that we can know the real value of products and make informed decisions so that we know prices have not been distorted.

Choice that creates competition and drives away the greedy bastards.

Interests that are aligned between the buyer and seller.

Ratigan is optimistic that we can bring back prosperity and break the grip of the Vampire Industries, but he warns of the rage that will follow when the greedy bastards are exposed by the weapons of VICI. He urges us not to use that rage for retribution, but to further unleash the forces of democracy and prosperity and innovation. As was demonstrated in 2011 by the protestors of the Arab

Spring, we now have a new weapon in the form of digital technology that links us together and allows us to expose the greedy bastards of the world to the light.

The Price of Inequality by Joseph Stiglitz

Stiglitz is a Nobel Prize winning economist, a member of Bill Clinton's Council of Economic Advisors, former chief economist for the World Bank, and is currently teaching at Columbia University. The originator of the term *one percent* that was the mantra of the Occupy Wall Street movement, he has studied the origins and consequences of inequality for over fifty years.

In the first chapter of his book, Stiglitz outlines the scope of inequality in the United States: a divided society; America no longer the land of opportunity; low chance of an individual to rise from the bottom to the top; and, polarization and decline of the middle class. These outcomes are the product of *inexorable market forces*, which over the past thirty years have resulted in a change from the top one percent receiving twelve percent of the national resources, to where in 2007, the average income of the top one percent was $1.3 million as opposed to the average income of the bottom twenty percent at $17,500. Stated differently, the top one percent was making in one week more than the bottom fifth made in a year. In the thirty years after World War II, America had grown together, with the bottom growing faster than the top. In the next thirty years, the top has grown faster and the bottom has declined.[7]

Stiglitz asserts that it was not only market distortions—incentives not to create new wealth but to take from others—that caused the inequality, but that government policies have also been central to the problem. It is not the American Economic engine that has failed to produce, but the way it has been run—giving benefits of growth to a small slice at the top and taking some from the bottom. In addition, he continues, the inequality in wealth far exceeds the inequality in income. Stiglitz asserts that the US has more inequality than any other advanced industrial nation and does less than any of the others to correct it. In fact, the inequality in the US is growing faster than in any other country.[8]

Under the marginal productivity theory to which most economists subscribe, the market rewards those with higher productivity through higher incomes. This theory justifies and explains some of the inequality. Stiglitz affirms that technology and scarcity, working through the ordinary laws of supply and demand, do play a role in shaping today's inequality. However, something else is at work as well, and that something is the government.

Market forces shape the degree of equality and government policies shape market forces. Typically, when sales fall, profit falls, but not in this economy, where the government has failed to ensure competitive markets and the market has become distorted.

Political forces also contribute to inequality because they set up and enforce the rules of the game for fair competition and the penalties for fraudulent practices; give out resources; redistribute income through taxes; alter the dynamics of wealth through inheritance tax, providing free public education, and health care; and determine to what degree the wealth and education of an individual will depend on that of the parent.

In our current political system, an inordinate amount of power goes to those at the top and many have used that power to limit distribution and shape the rules of the game in their favor to extract large gifts from the public. Stiglitz uses the term *rent seeking* and defines it as *individuals getting income not as a reward to creating wealth but by grabbing a large share of wealth that would otherwise have been produced without their effort.*[9]

This has created an economy and a society in which great wealth is amassed through rent seeking, sometimes through direct transfers from the public to the wealthy, more often through rules that allow the wealthy to collect 'rents' from the rest of society through monopoly power and other forms of exploitation, such as predatory lending and abusive credit card practices. These rents have moved dollars from the bottom and middle to the top and distorted the market to the advantage of some and to the disadvantage of others.[10]

Stiglitz fears that, under the current system, America may never regain its former status as the land of opportunity, where even the most humble citizen can rise to the top, or at least the middle, through hard work and initiative. However, he does outline a detailed solution to the problem of inequality, which boils down to the creation of government policies that curb excess at the top, reduce the practice of rent seeking, and level the economic playing field. From his years of research and study, Stiglitz is convinced that these solutions will strengthen rather than weaken the economy. As the wealth is redistributed more fairly through the alignment of private rewards and social rewards, assuring that returns received are equal to the benefits to society that the actions produced, the economy will grow and all will benefit.

A Home on the Field by Paul Cuadros

Cuadros, whose family immigrated to the US in 1960 from Peru, is an investigative reporter who moved to

Chatham County, North Carolina in 1999, after receiving an Alicia Patterson Foundation Fellowship to write about the impact of the large number of Latino poultry workers on rural towns in the South. While he was there, he became involved in an effort to establish and coach a soccer team at Jordan Matthews High School, in Siler City, an all-football town that resented the growing number of Latino youth pouring into the community.

The hostility toward the newcomers boiled over into an anti-immigrant rally led by ex-Klansman David Duke in February of 2000. Despite the odds, Cuadros worked for positive change, and in the end, not only got his soccer team, but over a three-year period, coached that team, *Los Jets*, to a state championship in soccer for Jordan Matthews.

Cuadros has been a positive force in promoting and publicizing the benefits of the Latino migration into towns like Siler City. When that migration began in the early 1990's, the town had suffered several major plant closings in textiles and furniture manufacturing. It had lost a thousand jobs, with a population of only five thousand. The youth were leaving to seek jobs in the larger cities and the median age, according to the 1990 census, was thirty-seven years. With the influx of Latinos, the median age in 2000 was thirty-one. The increased population revived business and growth.

The book provided a window into the issues of cultural and racial bias that stand in the way of creating a level playing field for Latino youths and their families as they seek to become working, contributing members in small rural communities across North Carolina. It was as well a window to my personal past, when in 1955, I moved with my family to Siler City, into the parsonage of the First Baptist Church, which sat directly across from the same two-story stone City Hall building where in February 2000, David Duke held his rally.

When we moved to Siler City, I was entering sixth grade at Paul Braxton Elementary School. We left there in 1958, in the middle of my ninth grade year at Jordan Matthews, home of the *Blue Phantoms*, an all-white high school where Friday night football was a community pastime. Who would have guessed that almost fifty years later, Jordan Matthews, now culturally and racially diverse, and known as the *JM Jets*, would make room for soccer and a state championship trophy, and would even be talking about converting the old Paul Braxton Field into a soccer complex.

A Time to Live: Seven Tasks of Creative Aging by Robert Raines

I have quoted this book extensively in previous chapters. The book has been helpful to me for its honest and encouraging treatment of how we can find meaning and fulfillment in life as we begin the *elder passage*, from middle age into the final stage of life that Raines has termed *The Elder Season*. Bill had copies of Raines' books *To Kiss the Joy* (1973), and *Creative Brooding: Readings to Provoke Thought and Trigger Action* (1977), and *Soundings* (1970) in his professional library; and, he often quoted from them in his sermons. This book was written twenty-some years later, when Raines was himself in his elder season.

Thinking Fast and Slow by Daniel Kahneman

The author is a winner of a Nobel Prize in Economic Sciences. The book is about the systems of our mind that drive thinking and help us make choices: System One, which is intuitive and fast, and System Two, which is logical, slow, and deliberate. I will have to admit that this book was a little bit over my head.

The Words of Jesus: A Gospel of the Sayings of Our Lord with Reflections by Phyllis Tickle

In this work, Tickle undertook to tease out the sayings of Jesus from the rest of the narrative in the gospels of Matthew, Mark, Luke, and John, and the book of Acts. Her goal was essentially to compile in one location all of the red-letter words that are used in various biblical translations to denote the actual sayings of Jesus. Tickle saw that task as important because those words as recorded and handed down to us were written by those who either knew Jesus or knew those who knew Him or, in the most extreme case, knew those who had known those who knew him. It also matters that those Sayings as recorded were accepted by the early, early Church *as accurate recordings*. Tickle shared her insight from her own study of the Sayings.

Her personal discovery was that these ancient words that have been passed down through the ages and preserved by the church as canon, still speak directly and without interpretation to the person of faith today, who is willing to focus upon them with both mind and heart. Tickle encourages the reader to confront the Sayings and to discover for him/herself the person of Jesus who comes down to us through those words, *for it is in the engagement and the pondering and the discovery that faith finds its proper exercise.*

Uncertainty by David Lindley

Phyllis Tickle references this book in *The Great Emergence.* She recommends it as required reading for the North American Christian who wants to grasp fully what the Great Emergence stands in juxtaposition to.[12] Lindley recounts how Werner Heisenberg's *uncertainty principle,* which states that there are physical limits to what we can know about sub-atomic particles, put him in direct opposition to Albert Einstein, with the scientist Niels Bohr mediating. Heisenberg's discovery would transcend the world of science and impact the general culture with the claim that there is no absolute truth, only truth relative to the perceiver.[13]

The Jewish Bible: A JPS Guide

This was one of the resources I used when I was working through an online course offered by Yale Divinity School, a survey of the Old Testament taught by Professor Christine Hayes.

NRSV Bible with Apocrypha

This version of the New Testament was required reading for the online course entitled *New Testament History and Literature,* taught by Dale Martin of Yale Divinity School.

Pedagogy of the Bible: An Analysis and Proposal by Dale
B. Martin

One of the assignments in the *New Testament*
course, to which I referred above, came from this book.
The author, who was also the teacher of the course, had
received a grant which he used to explore and report on
the methods of teaching biblical studies in seminaries and
divinity schools, as well as offer his own conclusions on the
type of curriculum that would best prepare seminarians for
Christian ministry. I was interested in the topic because
my son Robert was in his second year of divinity school at
Wake Forest University, and I had been thinking about
how his studies at Wake compared to the studies that Bill
had been exposed to at Southeastern Seminary back in the
late sixties.

From his interviews conducted at ten theological
institutions across the country, Martin found the dominant
method in the teaching of biblical studies to be historical
criticism. Although he acknowledges the importance of this
method, he asserts that students should be educated as
well in theological interpretation and in interpretation
theory itself. Students will spend their careers interpreting
the Bible for theological and ethical ends but, based on the
current course offerings at the ten seminaries under study,

they are not being trained sufficiently in how to think and speak articulately about theological interpretation. Martin argues that they need to learn to think *critically, self-consciously, and creatively about what sort of thing Scripture is.*[14]

They should be able to answer questions, such as *How do we interpret the text?* and *What are you doing when you interpret a text?* And, *Is the meaning in the text? The past? The author? In the reader?* [15]

Martin believes that students must be prepared to lead their future congregants from their childhood understandings of Scripture toward more complex and mature interpretations. For example, he suggests that one way Scripture can be understood is as a space we enter, something like a museum or sanctuary. When we read it alone or hear it read, it informs our imagination and reshapes us. This is much different from the notion of Scripture as a blueprint or list of rules to live by, which is a much more common interpretation.

Martin asserts that students will have difficulty moving beyond the historical meaning of Scripture, to include a wider range of interpretation, as long as the primary method of teaching biblical studies remains historical criticism.

Books for Pure Enjoyment

Cleopatra: A Life by Stacy Schiff

A well-written story that pieces together the facts and various historical accounts of the mysterious life of this ancient queen of Egypt.

A Game of Thrones: A Song of Ice and Fire by George RR Martin—referred to earlier in this chapter

A Clash of Kings: A Song of Ice and Fire by George RR Martin

A Storm of Swords: A Song of Ice and Fire by George RR Martin

A Feast for Crows: A Song of Ice and Fire by George RR Martin

Elizabeth I by Margaret George

Historical novel based on the life of Queen Elizbeth I and partially told from the perspective of Lettice Knollys, the queen's look-alike cousin and rival.

Caleb's Crossing by Geraldine Brooks

Historical novel about a man from Martha's Vineyard who was the first Native American graduate of Harvard.

James Madison and the Struggle for the Bill of Rights by
Richard Labunski

Recounts the struggle between Madison and Patrick
Henry in Virginia to ratify the Constitution.

Remarkable Creatures by Tracy Chevalier

Historical fiction based on the life of Mary Anning,
who lived in the early nineteenth century in the town of
Lyme Regis, on the south coast of England, where fossils
were abundant. She discovered the first complete
specimen of an ichthyosaur, a marine reptile about two
hundred million years old, and in the process became
acquainted with some of the great scientists of the time
who had begun to challenge the belief, held for one-
hundred-fifty years, that the earth was about six thousand
years old. This book is by the same author as *Girl with the
Pearl Earring*, which is a fictional account of the girl in the
painting of the same name, by Johannes Vermeer.

*Autobiography of Mark Twain: The Complete and
Authoritative Edition, Volume 1* Harriet Elinor Smith, Ed

Mark Twain made numerous attempts to write or
dictate his autobiography between 1870 and 1905, which
he never completed. In 1906, he began daily dictations

that he completed in 1909. However, he insisted that his autobiography remain unpublished until one hundred years after his death to ensure that he could hold to his commitment to tell the whole truth, without reservation. He told one interviewer that *A book that is not to be published for a century gives the writer a freedom which he could secure in no other way. In these conditions you can draw a man without prejudice exactly as you knew him and yet have no fear of hurting his feelings or those of his sons or grandsons.*[16]

Twain's adopted a method, which he declared should replace the traditional approach based on chronology and become the new model for autobiographical work, was *to start at no particular time of your life; wander at your free will all over your life; talk only about the thing which interests you for the moment; drop it the moment its interest threatens to pale, and turn your talk upon the new and more interesting thing that has intruded itself into your mind meantime.*[17]

The House I Loved by Sarah Key

A story about a woman living in the 1860's whose home and life were placed in jeopardy, as a result of Emperor Napoleon III and Baron Haussmann's renovations of Paris to make it a *modern city*.

The Scotish Prisoner by Diana Gabaldon

Historical novel set in London in 1760, about James Frazier, a Jacobite prisoner of war and Scottish Highlander who is called on to translate a letter written in an ancient Scottish language, which reveals a political conspiracy.

Distant Hours by Kate Morton

A gothic novel set in 1941, around Milderhurst Castle near London, the story revolves around events of World War II, when families from London sent their children into the countryside to live to be safe from the bombing.

The World According To Bertie by Alexander McCall Smith

By one of my favorite authors, this book is a part of the *44 Scotland Street* series, and is about a set of interesting characters who share a building of flats in Edinburgh. McCall Smith is a writer and professor emeritus at Edinburgh University.

The Double Comfort Safari Club by Alexander McCall Smith

McCall Smith was born in Zimbabwe and taught law at the University of Botswana. This book is from a delightful series called *No. 1 Ladies Detective Agency*, which features the owner of the agency, Mma Precious Ramotswe, and her assistant Mma Grace Makutsi.

Bringing Up Bebe by Pamela Druckerman

This book is by an American journalist and writer who along with her British husband, is raising her kids in Paris. When she observed that French children were *doing their nights* by three months, eating grown up food and sitting still in restaurants as toddlers, and playing without need for constant parent attention, she began a research project to discover the philosophy and principles of French child rearing.

The Sharper Your Knife the Less You Cry by Kathleen Flinn

The author writes about her experiences in 2003 when she attended cooking school in Paris and received a diploma from the Cordon Bleu Cooking School at the end of the year.

Afterword

Journey's End

We shall not cease from exploration and the end of all our exploring will be to arrive where we started and know the place for the first time. T.S. Eliot

The anniversary of my first year of retirement was soon approaching, and I began to reflect on my journey through the past twelve months. I had set out to discover how I would fill the forty plus hours in the workweek that the State of North Carolina returned to me to spend freely and at my own discretion after thirty years of a career as a public school educator. I also wanted to explore what I could do to live fully and purposefully as I travel through the elder passage of life, and to chronicle my experiences and findings along the way.

I began the year with a literal journey and discovered that travel would be one of the essential spices of life. On my trip to the UK, I drank in the exotic landscapes of Edinburgh and the Highlands of Scotland, infused with the beauty and awesomeness of the planet. I felt the strong pull of the tie that binds humankind, both now and through the ages, as I shouldered through the crowds in London to walk the historic paths, worn smooth by the feet of tourists like me who have come for centuries to experience the hustle and bustle and excitement of one of the world's most fascinating cities. As I ventured into new and different places over two thousand miles away from home, I was struck as I observed how similar we humans are in the performance of daily rituals like celebrating our sports victories, spending time with our families during leisure hours, and explaining the troubling aspects of our national histories to our children. It was comforting to realize how much more alike we are than different.

Sadly, the members of the human family are vastly different in terms of access to basic necessities and resources. This reality jolted us as we followed the news accounts of the burning and looting in Tottenham and as we saw evidence of the spread of vandalism when Robert and I passed through the heavily patrolled station in Birmingham on our way to Stratford-Upon-Avon. This was yet another example of the consequences reaped across the globe, resulting from the repression and deprivation of basic human needs in the process of protecting the resources of the privileged while ignoring the plight of the underprivileged.

The economic chasm between the *one percent* and the ninety-nine percent and the senseless inequity between *Haves* and *Have Not's* when there is plenty to go around, are problems of epic proportion. For years, I had seen the effects of those conditions as I struggled to level the educational playing field for my students living in poverty. However, it was in London where I woke up and made the connection between what was happening there and my own experiences.

My love for travel and exposure to other sites and cultures and languages grew during those twelve days in the UK, as did my feeling that there really is no place like home. The next two weekends, I reveled in the love of my family and celebrated important milestones in the lives of two of its very important members: my oldest son Todd, who turned forty and my Mother-in-law Margie, who turned ninety-two.

I journeyed next through the dust and cobwebs of my possessions, convinced that the organizing and de-cluttering of my physical space, would lighten my mental load and free me up to travel more easily into the elder season. It was a successful journey that left me energized and motivated to travel on, with a clean house to boot.

After that, I went off to fight the battle of the bulge and came back ten pounds lighter and full of optimism that

I would succeed in ultimately winning the war. In the month that followed, I set out to explore the boundaries of my literary talent, heard one of my favorite authors, blogged a bit, and published a small book of poems. At the end of that excursion, I realized that writing would become a key ingredient in the recipe for living that I was in the process of concocting.

In the winter months, my journey led me unwillingly into the valley of sorrows. As I began to spread my wings and fly out of it, I did so with greater sensitivity to the sorrows of others, as well as a commitment to use my own sorrow toward alleviating the causes of injustice and inequality around me. I began to envision how I could weave together the joys and sorrows in my life into a rich and textured tapestry of meaning. I sensed that these causes would become the focus of my work as I re-envisioned it.

In early spring, I made two wonderful side trips off the main road that I had intended to travel, just as I was heading back to work on my *Nonnie Project*. The first was the one on which I became hopelessly immersed for three weeks in online courses in New Testament and Old Testament that turned off the shuffle button and began to unscramble the Scriptures for me. The second came immediately on the heels of that, when I took off in search of my roots and wandered into an endless maze of information on Ancestry.com , causing me to lose all sense of time and space.

I emerged from that foray with a family history that is digitized and accessible to my children and grandchildren. In the process, I learned something about myself as well. I discovered that there are an infinite number of interests that I want to explore. Instead of being afraid that I will not be able to fill the hours of my remaining days, I am more afraid that I will not have enough days left to ponder even a fraction of those interests. I also *got psyched up* about learning German and traveling to Berlin to visit my grandfather's birthplace, and then realized that the responsible thing to do would be to learn Spanish first, a language that I could actually use to communicate with the Hispanic clients at Crisis Control Ministries where I volunteer weekly.

The land of books is one I visited more frequently and with greater duration throughout the year. It has been a wonderful place to go for diversion as well as for inspiration and edification. I have kept my Kindle near at hand for reading and an audio book in my car to listen to whenever I am out and about. I even have my Kindle synced to my smart phone so that I can read a few lines when I am waiting for an appointment or have a few minutes of down time. The books I read both inspire and intimidate me as I struggle to develop my own style and make my own way as a writer.

I began the year by tackling the goals that would bring immediate results, those that were concrete and attainable, and those that I could check off on a *To-Do list,* so to speak. It was a successful strategy for two reasons. For one, I gained a great sense of accomplishment from the completion of cleaning and de-cluttering and organizing all of my personal baggage, of addressing my weight, and of following through with a daily writing regimen, all in a relatively short period. The completion of those tasks energized me and boosted my confidence to tackle more complex tasks.

For the other reason, that day I walked out of my office last August, I was simply not ready emotionally or psychologically to confront some of the more abstract, open-ended questions that were swarming around in my mind, especially those related to my work and to my spiritual life. Contributing to a fragile psyche were the unresolved grief over my father's death and the impending loss of a brother-in-law and contemporary. Besides, it was hard as hell to accept the fact that I myself am getting old and have more years behind me than ahead. The initial impact of retirement was a splash of ice-cold water to the face, waking me up to that reality. Fortunately, the shock was temporary, and it began to wear off with each step I took to implement the goals and resolutions in my Retirement Project.

Thus, I progressed from an initial focus on concrete, structured, and time-referenced tasks in the early months, to a period of exploration and discovery of subjects that engaged my interests and attention in the winter months. By spring, I was ready to think about how I would re-define my work for the elder season. I discovered that the theme of leveling the playing field for disadvantaged youth, is one that has consistently played throughout the years in my song of work, and that I have a final note yet to complete in that melody.

Finally, in May, I dipped my oars into the waters of my spiritual and religious past in an effort to reconcile a love-hate relationship with the Church, and to determine its relevance to the world and to my life. I found that those waters run much deeper than I had imagined, and that I still bear wounds which have festered and have not yet healed. It has been helpful, by recalling and narrating key memories of those days, to bring them up into the light to examine and confront. However, I have concluded that the answers to my questions do not lie in the past; rather, they lie in the here and now.

I believe that answers will come in time, as I take baby steps to return to that part of the Church that served as my spiritual community until I dropped out of it twenty-some years ago. They will come as I seek to find my role in the emergence of a Christianity that will carry the message of God's love and justice for the entire world into the new millennium. It is an exciting time to be alive, and I, for one, hope to be around long enough to see what comes next.

I have travelled many miles, both literally and metaphorically, since the day almost a year ago now, that I walked out of my office into the hot summer air to begin my retirement. I did not find all of the answers that I was seeking in the course of those twelve short months, nor did I fulfill every one of my goals. However, I did *begin with the end in mind*. I did focus on the ten resolutions that I had identified as keys to happiness and fulfillment; and, as a result, I did discover a definite sense of meaning and accomplishment in my life that I will build upon as I continue my journey into the elder season.

It is my hope that in writing about my Retirement Project and how it came to be, others who are beginning their elder passage will be inspired to take time out to create their own projects and to embark on their own journeys for meaning and happiness. If you are among those who are about to retire, I can assure you that you will find it well worth the energy and effort. I can assure you as well that your project will be as different from mine as mine is from those of Gretchen Rubin and Robert Raines, and all of the others who inspired me. I predict that you will discover, as I have, that when it comes to the pursuit of happiness and fulfillment, retirement will always be a work in progress, a journey more than a destination.

Over the next decade, my generation of Baby Boomers will retire and pass through what for many will become an extended elder season, when compared to that of our parents and grandparents. We are the first massive demographic group to experience this phenomenon of increased longevity, and through our sheer numbers, we will dramatically change the perspective on aging in America. Whether that change will be a positive or negative one remains to be seen.

To ensure that our longer futures do not turn into *life sentences*, for ourselves, our children, and society in general, we will need to acquire the knowledge and learn the skills that will empower us to age with dignity and purpose. That will require us to get to work on creating fresh visions and constructing new models for retirement, and ultimately for successful aging. If our generation can pull that off, we will leave behind a legacy of positive change for our children and for our grandchildren.

The work will be challenging and downright hard; but, as my dad always said, *Old age is not for sissies!*

Acknowledgements

I am grateful to my family for their continuous love and support, as well as to the wider circle of friends, colleagues, and acquaintances who have enriched and enhanced my life in both the past and present. You have provided me with enough rich and interesting subjects to write about that I could fill a library with the volumes.

I want to thank Pam Bumgarner, for taking on the crucial but tedious task of reading and editing my manuscript with the eye of an English teacher.

Thanks as well to my cousin Beth and my sister Betsy, who were kind enough to review my early drafts about Nonnie, write down a few of their own stories of her, and encourage me to finish the memoir, which I intend to do.

Thanks to my son Todd for encouraging me to try my hand at self-publishing on Kindle, and to my sons John, Robert and Harry for the times they have listened to me read my anecdotes, sketches, and drafts upon which this book is based.

I especially want to thank my husband Bill, for supporting me as a fledgling author throughout the writing process, by reading and editing my drafts, and by offering gentle but honest feedback, which greatly improved the outcome of the book.

Notes

Introduction

1. Rubin, Gretchen. *The Happiness Project*.
2. Raines, Robert. *A Time to Live*.
3. Ibid., Loc.90.
4. Ibid., Loc. 973.
5. Sedensky, Matt. *Number of Centenarians is Booming in the United States*. HuffingtonPost.com, 26 Nov. 2011. Web. 17 Nov. 2012.
6. *Baptist Retirement Homes of North Carolina, Inc.* BRH.org. n.d. Web. 17 Nov 2012.
7. Sedensky, Matt. *Number of Centenarians is Booming in the United States*. HuffingtonPost.com, 26 Nov. 2011. Web. 17 Nov. 2012.

Chapter 1

1. This epic tale was difficult to summarize, and I found some help among the Amazon book reviews. *Fall of Giants*. Amazon.com.
2. I came across this information about the sculptor of the statue of John Bunyan that Robert and I visited in London at Speel, Bob. *Richard Garbe RA (1876-1957)*. Bob.Speel@tiscali.co.uk.

Chapter 2

1. Walsh, Peter. *It's All Too Much*. New York, 24.
2. Ibid., 26.
3. Silverstein, Shel. *Where the Sidewalk Ends*, 70-71.

Chapter 3

1. Chappell, Fred. *I Am One of You Forever,* 25.
2. Ibid., 93.
3. The poem, from Lewis Carroll's Alice in Wonderland is printed in Covey, Franklin. *The Seven Habits of Highly Effective People: Signature Program* , 35.
4. This was a quote from my uncle Schaefer's column in the *Greenville News*. It was about his brother Charlie, but it also described with eloquence our feeling of gratitude when Nonnie was finally released from her world of confusion as a victim of Alzheimer's. Kendrick, Schaefer. *Events Unfolded, and Charlie Watched and Lived."* Greenville News, 3E.

Chapter 4

1. This is a very helpful web site with many free resources. *Food and Fitness Journal.* Everydayhealth.com. Everyday Health Media, LLC. n.d. Web. 10 Nov. 2011.

Chapter 5

1. The poem entitled *Sweeping Up the Heart* by Emily Dickenson is printed in Raines, Robert. *A Time to Live: Seven Steps to Creative Aging*, 7.
2. Ibid., 29.

Chapter 6

1. The web site for the online religion courses in which I became engrossed is Martin, Dale. *Introduction to the New Testament.* OYC.Yale.edu. Many other courses are listed in the online catalog as well.
2. I found this site on Wikipedia to be very helpful in tracing my Poerschke relatives. *East Prussia.* Wikepedia.org. Wikimedia Foundations, Inc.

3. Ibid.
4. The online site that I used to trace my family history was Ancestry.com. Ancestry.com Internet Services. There are other sites, but this one boasts of having the most data.
5. Kendrick, Mattie Bryant. *My Dearest One*, 4.
6. The information about the Great Collinsville Mail Robbery is taken almost verbatim from an article written by K.L. Monroe, in a column entitled *As I See It*, in the Collinsville paper, no date attached. I also got some background information about the Shelton Brothers and the Charlie Berger gang from the IBEX archives storing information gathered from the Social History Project, East St. Louis Action Research, conducted in Spring of 1999, using monies provided from a Partnership Illinois grant, the East St. Louis Action Research, *Southern Illinois. Deals You Can't Refuse*. Eslarp.uiuc.edu.
7. Information from the 2010 census was drawn from *Hispanic Population 2010*. Census.gov.
8. Information about Spanish language learning programs can be found at *Learn Spanish*. Pimsleur.com; *Learn Spanish*. Rosettastone.com.; and, *Spanish Lesson 1*. Effectivelanguagelearning.com.
9. Essig, Debbie Wallace. "Patsy Ann. *Patsyann.net.*, first paragraph in Patsy Ann and Me.
10. Ibid.
11. *Doll Hospital*. dollsbydiane.net.

Chapter 7

1. The Malcolm Baldridge Award is given through the National Institute of Standards and Technology which is under the direction of the US Department of Commerce. Information about the Baldridge Performance Excellence Program as well as the names and contacts of the recipients, can be found

at nist.gov, which has a link to the Baldridge homepage.
2. The North Carolina Common Core Standards can be viewed on the NC Department of Instruction web site at Ncpublicschools.org. An explanation of the common core standards can be found at Governor.state.nc.us. 3 June 2010.
3. An outline of the new teacher evaluation process can be viewed at *North Carolina Teacher Evaluation Process.* Macon.k12.nc.us. n.d. Web. 10 May 2012.

Chapter 8

1. *Civil Rights Act of 1964.* Wikipedia.org.
2. *Voting Rights Act of 1965.* Core-online.org.
3. *Fair Housing Act.* Justice.gov. U.S.
4. McHorse, Claud. *Chronology of the SBC Takeover.* Mchorse.com/sbcchronology.htm. McHorse.com. n.d. Web. 5 May 2012.
5. Paige Patterson. Wikepedia.org.
6. Pressler: *Conservative Resurgence was Grassroots Movement.* Bpnews.net.
7. Hunter, Jeannine. *Fred Luter Elected First African-American Head of Southern Baptists.* Washingtonpost.com . 19 June 2012.
8. Information about the Alliance of Baptists can be found at Allianceofbaptists.org. Information about the Cooperative Baptist Fellowship can be found at thefellowship.info
9. Tickle, Phyllis. *The Great Emergence.*
10. Ibid., 16
11. Ibid., 25
12. Ibid., 46
13. Ibid., 65
14. Ibid., 125 in footnote 1.
15. Ibid., 124.
16. Ibid., 126.
17. Ibid., 152

18. Ibid., 153
19. Ibid., 154

Chapter 9

1. *George RR Martin*. Wikepedia.org.
2. Clemmons, Hardy. *Saying Goodbye*, 59.
3. Ratigan, Dylan. Greedy Bastards, 11.
4. Ibid.
5. Ibid.
6. Ibid.
7. Stiglitz, Joseph. *The Price of Inequality*, 10.
8. Ibid. 74.
9. Ibid.
10. Ibid., 266.
11. Tickle, Phyllis. *The Words of Jesus*.
12. Ibid., 69.
13. Ibid., 43.
14. Martin, Dale. Pedagogy of the Bible, 64.
15. Ibid.
16. Autobiography of Mark Twain, HE Smith Ed., 2.
17. Ibid., 1.

Works Cited

Ancestry.com. *Ancestry.com Internet Services. n.d. Web.5 March 2012.*

*ACRE: Accountability and Curriculum Reform Effort.*Ncpublicschools.org. n.d. Web.5 May 2012.

Aronne, Louis J.*The Skinny: On Losing Weight Without Being Hungry.* New York:Broadway Books, 2009. Print.

2008 Awards Recipients. Nist.gov. U. S.Department of Commerce. 25 November 2008. Web. 4 April 2012.

Baptist Retirement Homes of North Carolina, Inc. BRH.org. n.d. Web. 17 Nov 2012.

Bonanno, George A .*The Other Side of Sadness:What the New Science of Bereavement Tells Us About Life After Loss.* New York: Perseus Books, 2009. Kindle edition.

Brooks, Geraldine.*Caleb's Crossing.*New York: Penguin Audio,2011.CD.

Bunyan, John.*A Pilgrim's Progress from This World to That.* Amazon Digital Services, September 14, 2011.Kindle edition.

Chappell, Fred.*I Am One of You Forever.* Baton Rouge: Louisiana State University Press,1985. Print.

Chevalier, Tracy.*Burning Bright.* New York: Penguin Audio,2007.CD.

Civil Rights Act of 1964. Wikipedia.org. Wikimedia Foundation, Inc. 8 Nov.2012. Web. 5 May 2012.

Conroy, Pat.*Prince of Tides.* Boston:Houghton Mifflin,1986. Print.

---. *Beach Music.*New York:Doubleday, 1995. Print.

Covey, Franklin.*The 7 Habits of Highly Effective People:Signature Program* .China: Franklin Covey, 2005.

De Rosnay, Tatiana.*The House I Loved.* New York: MacMillan Audio, 2012. CD.

Diane's Doll Hospital. Dollsbydiane.com. n.d. Web. 25 March 2012.

Druckerman, Pamela. *Bringing Up Bebe.* New York: Random House Audio, 2012. CD.

East Prussia. Wikepedia.org. Wikimedia Foundations, Inc. 21 Oct. 2012. Web. 2 March 2012.

Edgerton, Clyde. *Walking Across Egypt.* Chapel Hill: Algonquin Books, 1987.

Education Criteria for Performance Excellence. Nist.gov. U.S. Department of Commerce. 27 August 2009. Web.4 April 2012.

Essig,Debbie Wallace.*Patsy Ann.*Patsyann.net. World Press. n.d. Web.3 March 2012.

*Fair Housing Act.*Justice.gov. U.S. Department of Justice. n.d. Web. 5 May 2012

Fall of Giants. Amazon.com. Amazon.com., Inc. n.d. Web. 25 June 2012.

Follette, Ken. *Fall of Giants*. New York: New American Library, 2010. Print

Food and Fitness Journal. Everydayhealth.com. Everyday Health Media, LLC. n.d. Web. 10 Nov. 2011

Gabaldon, Diana. *The Scottish Prisoner*. New York: Recorded Books, 2011. CD.

George, Margaret. *Elizabeth I*. New York: Penguin Audio, 2011. CD.

George RR Martin. Wikepedia.org. Wikimedia Foundations, Inc. 5 Nov. 2012. Web. 13 Nov. 2012.

Graves, Donald. *Teachers and Children at Work*. Portsmouth: Heinemann, 1983.

Gregory, Philippa. *The Lady of the Rivers*. New York: Audioworks, 2011. CD.

---. *The Red Queen*. New York: Audioworks, 2010. CD.

---. *The White Queen*. New York: Audioworks, 2009. CD.

Hart, John. *The Last Child*. New York: St. Martin's Press, 2009. Print.

Hispanic Population 2010. Census.gov. U.S. Department of Commerce. May 2011. Web. 3 March 2012.

Hunter, Jeannine. *Fred Luter Elected First African-American Head of Southern Baptists*. Washingtonpost.com . Washington Post. 19 June 2012. Web. 13 Nov. 2012.

Learn Spanish. Pimsleur.com. Simon and Schuster. n.d. Web. 3 March 2012.

Learn Spanish. Rosettastone.com. Rosetta Stone, Ltd. n.d. Web. 3 March 2012.

Kahneman, Daniel. *Thinking, Fast and Slow*. New York: Random House, 2011. CD.

Kendrick, Schaefer. *Events Unfolded, and Charlie Watched and Lived*. Greenville News 14 June. 1992, Greenville, 3E. Print.

Kendrick, Mattie Bryant. *My Dearest One*. Greenville, Hiott Press, 1955.

King, Mona Reed. *Patsy Ann: Her Happy Times*. Rand McNally, 1936.

Labunski, Richard. *James Madison and the Struggle for the Bill of Rights*. New York: Recorded Books LLC, 2006. CD

Lindley, David. *Uncertainty: Einstein, Heisenberg, Bohr, and the Struggle for the Soul of Science*. New York: Random House, Inc., 1927. Kindle edition.

Martin, Dale. *Introduction to New Testament*. OYC.Yale.edu. Yale University. n.d. Web. 2 Feb.2012.

---. *Pedagogy of the Bible: An Analysis and Proposal*. Louisville: Westminster John Knox Press, 2008. Kindle edition.

Martin, George R.R. *A Game of Thrones: A Song of Ice and Fire.* New York: Bantam Books, 1996. Kindle edition.

---. *A Clash of Kings. A Song of Ice and Fire.* New York: Bantam Books, 1999. Kindle edition.

---. *A Storm of Swords. A Song of Ice and Fire.* New York: Bantam Books, 2000. Kindle edition.

---. *A Feast for Crows. A Song of Ice and Fire.* New York: Bantam Books, 2005. Kindle edition.

McCall Smith, Alexander. *The Perils of Morning Coffee.* New York: Recorded Books LLC, 2011. CD.

---. *A Conspiracy of Friends.* New York: Recorded Books LLC, 2012. CD.

---. *The Limpopo Academy of Private Detection.* New York: Recorded Books LLC, 2012. CD.

---. The Unbearable Lightness of Scones. New York: Recorded Books LLC, 2012. CD.

McLain, Paula. *Paris Wife.* New York: Ballentine Books, 2011. Print

McCullough, David. *The Greater Journey.* New York: Simon and Shuster, 2011. Kindle edition.

McHorse, Claud. *Chronology of the SBC Takeover.* Mchorse.com/sbcchronology.htm. McHorse.com. n.d. Web. 5 May 2012

Morris, Edmund. *Colonel Roosevelt.* New York: Random House, 2010. Print.

Morton, Kate. *The Distant Hours.* Grand Haven: Bolinda Publishing Pty Ltd, 2010. CD.

Mosse, Kate. *Labyrinth.* New York: Penguin Audio, 2006. CD.

---. *Winter Ghosts.* New York: Putnam and Sons, 2009. Print.

New Revised Standard Version Holy Bible with Apocrypha. New York: HarperCollins Publishers, 2006. Kindle edition.

North Carolina Adopts Common Core State Standards. Governor.state.nc.us. Office of the Governor. 3 June 2010. Web. 5 May 2012.

North Carolina Teacher Evaluation Process. Macon.k12.nc.us. n.d. Web. 10 May 2012.

Paige Patterson. Wikepedia.org. Wikimedia Foundations, Inc. 26 Sept. 2012. Web. 13 Nov. 2012.

Pressler: Conservative Resurgence was Grassroots Movement. Bpnews.net. Baptist Press of the Southern Baptist Convention. 30 March 2004. Web. 5 May 2012.

Raines, Robert. *A Time to Live: Seven Steps to Creative Aging.* New York: Penguin Putnam, Inc., 1998. Print.

Ratigan, Dylan. *Greedy Bastards.* New York: Simon and Shuster, 2012. Kindle edition.

Rowling, J.K. *Harry Potter and the Sorcerer's Stone*. New York: Scholastic, 1997. Print.

---. *Harry Potter and the Deadly Hallows.* New York: Scholastic, 2007.

Rubin, Gretchen. *The Happiness Project: Or Why I Spent a Year Trying to Sing in the Morning, Clean my Closets, Fight Right, Read Aristotle, and Generally Have More Fun.* New York: Harper Collins Publishers, 2009. Kindle edition.

Shakespeare, William. *The Tragedy of King Richard III*. HTML version prepared by Jeseph Loewenstein, M.D. Kindle edition.

Schiff, Stacy. *Cleopatra: A Life*. New York: Hatchett Audio, 2011. CD.

Sedensky, Matt. *Number of Centenarians is Booming in the United States*. HuffingtonPost.com. HuffPost News 26 April 2011. Web. 17 Nov 2012.

Silverstein, Shel. *Where the Sidewalk Ends*. Newy York: Harper Collins, 1974. Print.

Southern Illinois: Deals You Can't Refuse. Eslarp.uiuc.edu. East St. Louis Action Research History Project. n.d. Web. 2 Feb. 2012.

Spanish Lesson 1. Effectivelanguagelearning.com. Effective Language Learning. n.d. Web. 3 March 2012.

Speel, Bob. *Richard Garbe RA (1876-1957).* Bob.Speel@tiscali.co.uk. Talk Talk Group. n.d. Web. 25 June 2012.

Stiglitz, Joseph. *The Price of Inequality.* New York: W.W. Norton and Company, 2012. Kindle edition.

Stillerman, Katherine P. *Exemplary Middle School Principals.* 1992.

Tally, Beth. *The Beacon.* Pittsbugh: Rose Dog Books, 2007. Print.

The Autobiography of Mark Twain, vol. 1. Edited by Harriet Elinor Smith. Berkley: University of California Press, 2010. Kindle edition.

The Jewish Bible: JPS Guide. Philadelphia: The Jewish Publication Society, 2008. Kindle edition.

Tickle, Phyllis. *The Great Emergence.* Grand Rapids: Baker Books, 2008. Kindle edition.

---. *The Words of Jesus: A Gospel of the Sayings of Our Lord with Reflections.* San Francisco: Jossey-Bass, 2008. Kindle edition.

Voting Rights Act of 1965. Core-online.org. Congress of Racial Equality. n.d. Web. 5 May 2012.

Walsh, Peter. *It's All Too Much.* New York: Free Press, 2007. Kindle edition.

Westberg, Granger E. *Good Grief.* Minneapolis: Fortress Press, 1971. Print.

Made in the USA
Lexington, KY
14 May 2015